Successful Community
Leadership

Successful Community Leadership

A Skills Guide for Volunteers and Professionals

John E. Tropman

NASW PRESS

National Association of Social Workers
Washington, DC

Josephine A. V. Allen, PhD, ACSW, *President*
Josephine Nieves, MSW, PhD, *Executive Director*

Jane Browning, *Director, Member Services/Publications*
Nancy A. Winchester, *Executive Editor*
Christina A. Davis, *Senior Editor*
Patricia D. Wolf, Wolf Publications, Inc., *Project Manager*
Ronald W. Wolf, *Copy Editor*
Elizabeth Reynolds, *Proofreader*
Louise R. Goines, *Proofreader*
Sandi Schroeder, *Indexer*

First impression September 1997
Second impression June 1998

**Library of Congress
Cataloging-in-Publication Data**

Tropman, John E.
    Successful community leadership: a skills guide for volunteers
    and professionals / John E. Tropman.
        p.   cm.
    Includes bibliographical references and index.
    ISBN 0-87101-285-5
    1. Community organization—United States. 2. Community
    leadership—United States. 3. Decision-making, Group—United
    States. I. Title.
HN90.C6T75   1997
361.2'5—dc21   97-30569
                                                        CIP

Printed in the United States of America.

Contents

Preface

A *community* is a group that has unity through some common elements. These sometimes overlapping elements can be geographic location, ethnic identification, or an affiliation or place of work (for example, the university community). Each community shares a sense of common fate as well.

Community decision making involves an attempt by community members, often with the help of community organizers, to make decisions that will improve the community's condition. A hallmark of the community organization and decision-making process is that the community decides which direction it wants to go and the projects it wants to undertake. However, community citizens often lack the skills to deal with elements of decision making or do not know what to do in community decision-making groups.

The process of working together in a community is complex (Rothman, Erlich, & Tropman, 1995; Tropman, Erlich, & Rothman, 1995) and involves the sharing of information. Although information sharing can be done using computers (with techniques called "groupware"), face-to-face exchange is still needed, because computers cannot share emotions (although "flaming"—angry, sometimes obscene electronic mail messages—is one inappropriate approach to emotional expression) (Keegan, 1995). The normative bases for decision legitimization (extensiveness of and depth of preference, implementation responsibility, expertise, and the preferences of those with power), their simultaneous presence of the norms, and differential weighting mean that group decision management is a necessity for both community professionals and volunteers. This book is designed to help everyone interested in community decision making do a better job.

What does "better" mean in this context? It means that decisions are made in a timely fashion. A good decision made too late is the same as no decision at all; it is a nondecision—a sort of "passive aggression" at the community level. Groups that never do anything soon lose their membership. Furthermore, decisions can be placed along a qualitative continuum that includes poor, good, and excellent ones. High-quality decision making occurs when a community interest is identified, circulated, and incorporated into the decision. For this to happen, good techniques, courage, and good will are required. The techniques in this book will be helpful in the community decision-making process and in the group process at work, church, or school. The book draws on the experience of community groups and leaders from around the country, including Pittsburgh; Chicago; Boston; Ann Arbor and Glen Arbor, Michigan; and Madison, Wisconsin, and shares the benefits of their wisdom.

Using This Guide

How to use this book For students and community facilitators, a read-through of this book is appropriate if you have the time. Several sections refer to the things a community worker might do (for example, staff duties is discussed in one place; meeting organizing is found in another). However, one needs to know the appropriate roles of the citizen leader in the different leadership positions. Many people have leadership interest and the ability to engage others but have no idea what leaders are supposed to do. Professional and student community facilitators can help educate a community in this regard using the information from this book. A couple of other suggestions are offered on how to best use this book.

Skim Through It

First, skim through the book, becoming familiar with the parts and chapters. Mark places of interest to yourself or others by folding over or placing a colored tag on a page. Different colors might be used to mark different kinds of information. Notes or selections for your use can poke out the top; those for others can poke out the side.

Skim

Read Relevant Sections

Read relevant sections in detail. Some of this book's information will be immediately applicable to your group process. A chairperson should read the section on chairpersons; a member should read the section on members.

Read

Adopt Group Guidelines

A step toward developing public procedures is to review this book at an early group meeting and adopt it as a guideline for the community process. That adoption means that the group supports the general ideas, orientations, and principles (for example, the group would support the principles that govern productive community processes and a particular structure for handling meetings). Many groups adopt some procedural guide—*Robert's Rules of Order* (1970) is common. However, *Robert's Rules* is narrowly focused and mostly concerned with the introduction of motions at large meetings. The procedures in this book address the widest compass of community interest.

Adopt

Questions? Readers can contact me with any questions: John E. Tropman, University of Michigan, 313-764-1817, or tropman@umich.edu. My home page has links to many of the Web sites mentioned in this book: http://www-personal.umich.edu/~tropman/commlead.html.

References

Keegan, P. (1995, October 22). The office that Ozzie built. *New York Times Magazine*, pp. 49–51.

Robert, H. M. (1970). *Robert's rules of order* (revised by S. C. Robert). Glenview, IL: Scott, Foresman.

Rothman, J., Erlich, J., & Tropman, J. E. (1995). *Strategies of community intervention*. Itasca, IL: F. E. Peacock.

Tropman, J. E., Erlich, J., & Rothman, J. (1995). *Tactics for community intervention*. Itasca, IL: F. E. Peacock.

Introduction

Professor John E. Tropman is nationally and internationally known for his work in theorizing and conceptualizing the issues related to community leadership. This book is merely the latest in a series of publications focusing on community organizing, group dynamics, and effective decision making. Tropman's publications have always dealt with significant social issues, and *Successful Community Leadership* is no exception. In fact, his present subject matter seems to me to be of vital importance for the future direction of society.

Social services in the United States are undergoing a seismic shift, as "welfare as we know it" indeed comes to an end, and many other social programs change. Some analysts applaud the recent changes, while others lament them. But both sides agree that social services are changing profoundly, as society redefines who is responsible for providing assistance to those in need. In the past, the federal government directly administered many social services, but these same services today are increasingly the purview of state and local governments and community organizations. These organizations are thus finding themselves in new partnerships, with new responsibilities. The new collaborations are fraught with potential pitfalls, because too often the team members—volunteers, civil servants, and government officials—do not possess the skills needed to work together effectively. Even with the best intentions on all sides, collaborations still fail if there is not a sufficient knowledge base to grant team members insight into the roles played by other organizations and their institutional priorities. *Successful Community Leadership* will provide needed insight into the characteristic composition and operation of community organizations.

Volunteers have long played a central role in community organizations. Professionals and volunteers must learn how to function effectively as a team both within community organizations and in partnership with other agencies. *Successful Community Leadership* will be a resource for all members of the public–private collaborations that will become increasingly prevalent; in fact, when Tropman first discussed this project with me, I felt that one of its strengths would be the dual focus on volunteers and professionals. Both sometimes have different perspectives, skills, backgrounds, and agendas, but they need to learn to work together effectively to meet common goals. This process is not only incredibly complex, as Tropman points out; it also is one that is negotiated every day.

Volunteerism has many beneficial effects, including creating and reinforcing a powerful sense of accomplishment and self-determination. Working together in community organizations can be a wonderfully empowering process for both volunteers and professionals as individuals learn that despite their differences they can work together to make a real difference in their community. In recent years, there has been increasing emphasis on the impact that volunteers can have on the quality of life within a neighborhood and the nation's children. For example, at the President's Summit for America's Future held in Philadelphia in April 1997, President Clinton; General Colin Powell; former Presidents Bush, Carter, and Ford; and former First Lady Nancy Reagan, among others, discussed ways that private citizens and organizations can take the initiative to transform their own communities. The President's Summit outlines many laudable goals, but to make them a reality we will need well-trained, strongly organized, and self-aware community organizations. There is a necessity for work such as Tropman's that discusses the skills needed for training and organizing volunteers at the local level. In *Successful Community Leadership*, Tropman discusses theoretical approaches to community organizing, but he also addresses the reality of community leadership to illuminate real-life problems and issues. One great academic peril is a publication that is beautifully written, flawlessly reasoned, and extremely clever—but that has little relevance and elicits little interest outside of academia. Tropman has wisely chosen to make his work highly relevant for and accessible to active practitioners, so that it can have an impact on many lives.

Successful Community Leadership is an easy-to-use source of information for anyone working for or with community organizations. It covers a range of relevant issues, including group decision-making processes, conflict resolution, the roles of committee chairpersons and members, differing work and learning styles, consumer engagement strategies, documentation and reporting, and electronic resources. Tropman's conclusions are clearly of considerable interest to community organizers, but they also are enormously helpful to anyone who ever works on a project as part of a group—which is nearly everyone. I found his elucidation of interpersonal dynamics with meetings enlightening and relevant to my own workplace, and I can imagine many more situations in which it would be useful.

Paula Allen-Meares, PhD, LCSW
Dean and Professor
School of Social Work
University of Michigan
Ann Arbor

Acknowledgments

This book is the product of many who deserve special mention. First is the W. K. Kellogg Foundation, especially Helen Grace and Pat Babcock. Their vision was one of community decision making, and the Community Health Models of Michigan is an expression of their vision. I was privileged to have a role in working with those model communities, and portions of this book grew out of that early work.

A special mention goes to my late father Elmer J. Tropman of the Forbes Fund and The Pittsburgh Foundation. Our many discussions about how foundations could assist in the community decision-making process shaped and improved every page of this work.

Pam Paul-Shaheen and Chuck Maynard are community workers par excellence who contributed ideas, support, and encouragement. Mary Cohen's suggestions on format were particularly helpful. Dan Madaj and Lesa Ball offered extraordinary skill and dedication, producing draft after draft, reformatting, updating, and adding editorial wisdom. Jessica Schenk did outstanding work (see appendix 1) in providing information to readers on how to obtain materials about their local community through the public library system and the Internet. Jessica taught me things about the library I thought I already knew but did not; she also taught me about the Internet, the World Wide Web, and online searching. Jessica developed my home page and linked other Internet sites that might be of most use. Carla Parry did great work (see appendix 2) in providing a case application of the materials discussed in this book.

Special thanks go to the citizens of the many communities in which I have worked—Pittsburgh; Chicago; Boston; Ann Arbor, Michigan; and Glen Arbor, Michigan; and many others—whose relentless demands for "useful stuff" were always at the forefront of my thinking. Community issues ranged from dioxin dumping in a local creek to "gold coast and slum" neighborhoods to downtown development to battles between developers and conservationists over wetlands. The communities provided laboratories where I could try techniques, observe results, reformulate approaches, and try again.

I thank the students at the School of Social Work, University of Michigan; Boston College; and the School of Social Service Administration, University of Chicago and others involved in community organization who read portions of this book, commented, and added their insights.

I could not end without a mention of Paula Allen-Meares, dean of the School of Social Work, University of Michigan. Every project has its snags, and this one was no exception. Paula was unfailing in her commitment to the idea that this book was useful and necessary. She provided understanding, encouragement, support, and occasional helpful intervention in the larger system. She is a true executive champion.

Part 1
Taking Leadership in Community Groups

A s Alexis De Tocqueville pointed out in *Democracy in America* (1841), America's backbone is the association and gathering of citizens to pursue personal and social good. This impetus is a part of our culture.

Such associations do not work by themselves; rather, they are opportunities for citizen leaders to guide the community. Community leadership is taken largely through such organizations as civic groups, action groups, boards of voluntary agencies, neighborhood groups, interest groups, and self-help groups. Through this latticework of groups and their interconnections, communities do their work.

Such associations often need assistance. Sometimes community organizers assist the community with issues of cohesion, recognizing that there are common issues. Other times community workers help the community that has cohesion become better at what it does. In addition, community workers assist capable communities to become better at community work, striving toward the goal of competent community decision making.

Community group leadership is available for both citizens and professionals. Part 1 of this book attends to the issues of leadership roles, addressing common problems, examining the jobs of group chairpersons and members, and discussing the responsibilities of groups themselves.

Reference

De Tocqueville, A. (1841). *Democracy in America.* New York: Langley.

Chapter 1

Obstacles to and Guidelines for Working Together in Community Development

Community enhancement involves bringing people together to improve lives and opportunities. Although every individual has his or her own interests, each of us sometimes seeks to act on behalf of the entire community or to express a trusteeship and stewardship function for the whole rather than just our part. Frequently, enacting stewardship involves elements of community decision making. This chapter discusses both obstacles to and ground rules for successful community decision making.

Enacting community trusteeship

Obstacles to Effective Group Decision Making

Many barriers exist to achieving high-quality decisions that advance the interests of the community as a whole. Some of these complications are the result of "rancorous conflict"—conflict that goes on and on (Gamson,

Common problems in community groups

1966). These are the difficult ones. Many others are less complicated and can be fixed more easily. However, if not attended to, minor problems can derail the community decision-making process. There are three types of problems: problems of procedure, problems of process, and problems of people.

Problems of Procedure

Procedural problems

Sometimes a community group has not set procedures that involve all stakeholders, which causes several problems. There are two problems worth noting here.

Iron Law of Oligarchy

Iron law of oligarchy

Political analyst Robert Michels (1876–1936) proposed that, over time, groups tend to be run by a small elite—an oligarchy (Michels, 1949). In community leadership this danger is always lurking, because the small elite enjoys its power. The political groups Michels wrote about were socialist in orientation, striving to bring about a more egalitarian society. However, equality and participation cannot be brought about by exclusion and elitism. (For more on Michels, see Linz, 1964.) There should be a process through which all members of the group take turns at leadership.

Single-Issue Individualism

Single-issue individualism

American society is individualistic (Reisman, 1954). This tendency, paradoxically, affects groups as well. In a community context, single-issue groups want exactly and only what they want regardless of the effect on others. There is no culture of community for them. Such groups often are the way they are because repeated problems of community process have eroded trust. Community leadership should seek to work with these groups as much as possible to rebuild trust.

Problems of Process

Sometimes the decision-making process becomes mired and twisted, and problems arise. Several kinds of bad results have been identified by writers in the field, some ancient and some modern. I will mention some of the most famous. This book provides techniques that help avoid these adverse outcomes.

Process problems

Folly

Barbara Tuchman developed the idea of folly in her book *The March of Folly* (1984). Folly occurs when a community picks a bad direction, but the community is not just making poor decisions. Other criteria must be met: general alternatives were available; a clear set of voices articulated these other options; and the decisions occurred over time (so it was not the result of one person). Two examples are the Trojan horse and the Vietnam War.

Folly

In the case of the Trojan horse, the Greeks were besieging the city of Troy. They hit on the strategy of constructing a huge wooden horse and hiding an attack team inside. The army then withdrew, leaving the horse at the gates of the city. The Trojans came out to find the horse and debated what to do about it. Suggestions included burning the horse or throwing it into the sea. The Trojans decided to bring the horse (and the attack team) into the city. After dark, the attack team emerged and opened the gates to the Greek army, who destroyed the city. As a community, Troy did not have good decision-making procedures.

Vietnam is another example where the decision making continues to be re-examined. The American government pushed ahead in its war effort when domestic support was very mixed. The war caused dissension and created cleavages in the country.

Group Think

Group think   Some conflict is necessary in community development work, because differences that never surface work in corrosive, nonpublic ways. *Group think* refers to making agreements under conditions of high cohesion, where no one wants to disturb the peace (Janis, 1983). Group think frequently occurs when a powerful individual puts pressure on a group to influence a decision. Group members acquiesce, fearful that they might be punished in some way or are simply not willing to take on that powerful individual. The agreement is false, however, because the minute the meeting ends individuals other than the powerful promoter are usually complaining among themselves. Sabotage may begin right away.

There are several components of group think (adapted from Janis, 1983):

- *Incomplete survey of alternatives.* Group discussion is limited to a few courses of action without a survey of the full range of alternatives.
- *Incomplete survey of objectives.* The group does not survey the objectives to be fulfilled and the values implicated by the choice.
- *Failure to examine the risks of the preferred choice.* The group fails to re-examine the course of action initially preferred by most members from the standpoint of the nonobvious risks and drawbacks that were not considered when it was originally evaluated.
- *Failure to reappraise initially rejected alternatives.* The group neglects courses of action initially evaluated as unsatisfactory, spending little or no time discussing whether they have overlooked gains that are not obvious.
- *Poor information search.* The group makes little or no attempt to obtain information from experts who can

supply sound estimates of gains and losses expected from alternative courses of action.

- *Selective bias in processing information.* The group likes facts that support what the members want to do and spends time discussing those facts; the group tends to ignore evidence of a contrary nature.

- *Failure to work out contingency plans.* The group spends little time deliberating how the chosen policy might be hindered by bureaucratic inertia or political sabotage; thus, the group fails to work out contingency plans.

Brute Think

Brute think is a term I use to explain the situation in which groups think they can bulldoze their way to a solution by "just keeping at it." Instead of engaging in "problem bracketing"—setting the difficult issue aside—they hammer away at one solution until members will accept almost anything to get out of the room.

Brute think

Abilene Paradox

The Abilene paradox was developed by Jerry Harvey (1974), who tells the story about a group of people in a car without air conditioning about an hour outside of Abilene on a hot day. Somehow, the group decides to go to Abilene for lunch. They travel a long way in an uncomfortable automobile in the blistering heat. The lunch is awful. On the way back, the group discovers that no one actually wanted to go to Abilene for lunch. The Abilene paradox has come to refer to those kinds of community decisions in which no one wanted to make the decision, but everyone somehow fell into it.

Abilene paradox

Garbage Can Model of Community Choice

Michael Cohen and others (Cohen, March, & Olson, 1972) argued that communities have four types of people. One kind is *problem knowers*—those who know

Garbage can model

the problems faced by individuals and the community. Ministers, doctors, and lawyers are problem knowers. A second type are *problem solvers*—creative individuals who know how to come up with ideas for solving problems and getting things done. They may not, however, know the community's problems. A third group are *resource controllers*—people who control important community resources. They always need to be involved. Finally, there are *decision makers looking for work*—individuals who can bring together disparate elements of a community and help them work together. Most of the time these people are assembled at random, as if thrown into a garbage can. For high-quality decisions to be made, communities must have all of these types of individuals involved in the process in the same room at the same time. Thus, in constructing task forces and steering committees, organizers should strive to include the four types of people.

Defensive Routines

Defensive routines

Defensive routines, an idea developed by Harvard University's decision analyst Chris Argyris (1985), refer to a situation in a group where certain topics are never discussed, and the reasons the topics are never discussed are never discussed either. Such routines may come into play in a community decision-making setting, for example, when a powerful member always gets his or her way. This event can never be discussed nor can approaches to discussing it be discussed.

Rube Goldberg Construction and Occam's Razor

Rube Goldberg construction

In the Rube Goldberg construction, complexity is seen as positive. In community decision making, faulty process often leads to overinclusion of approaches and steps, thus creating extra work and threatening implementation. A decision that is too complicated to work is the same as making no decision.

William of Occam, a clergyman who lived in the early 14th century, formulated a rule for judging between competing mathematical proofs. Occam's razor, useful in community work, was that simpler was better; the proof with the fewest steps was the winner (Jones, 1952). **Occam's razor**

Zeno's Paradox
Zeno, a 5th-century B.C. Greek philosopher, pointed out that if one approaches a wall and covers half the remaining distance with each step, one will never reach the wall. In community decision making, a group may get closer and closer but never actually make the decision. Zeno's paradox is a type of decision avoidance psychosis. **Zeno's paradox**

The Nondecision, or the Boiled-Frog Phenomenon
Nondecision occurs when communities allow events to proceed without taking action and thus find themselves, in a sense, dead. In the boiled-frog metaphor, I use a high school science experiment. Put a frog in a petri dish of water and slowly heat it over a Bunsen burner. The frog eventually boils to death. Why doesn't the frog jump out? The answer lies in the concept of the "just noticeable difference." In many communities, change is happening slowly. Community leadership sometimes does not perceive the changes and thus fails to come together and act. **Boiled-frog phenomenon**

A community-based strategic planning process project can help a community avoid becoming a boiled frog. The planning process can identify and determine ways to cope with change.

Problems of People

Several personality types can hinder the decision-making process. Harvard economist Amartya Sen (1992) has pointed out that there are always individuals who **People problems**

Spoilers,
partisans,
politicians,
novices

would prefer to lower other's gain than raise their own. Those individuals are *spoilers*.

Partisans are unable to set aside their emotional, personal, or stakeholder issues to view the community as a whole and determine what might be appropriate for it. When they do get together, these single-issue individualists fuse into single-issue groups. Zealots or "true believers" are extreme cases (Hoffer, 1951).

Politicians seek to use every community process to advance their careers. They may have political aspirations or may be engaging in social climbing.

Novices do not have the necessary experience and background to function in a community group. The tendency is to remove these individuals from the process. Paradoxically, even though an individual is ineffective, attempts to remove him or her build sympathy.

Elements of Good Community Process

To be successful, the community decision-making process should possess certain factors. Primary among these are inclusiveness, trustworthiness, viability, validity, and reliability.

Inclusiveness,
trustworthiness,
viability,
validity,
reliability

- *Inclusiveness* means that a wide range of people are involved in the process (see chapter 2).
- *Trustworthiness* means that the meetings one attends are the real ones; no backroom decisions have overtaken the public process.
- *Viability* means that decisions made in such forums stand up and do not erode over time, suggesting that the decisions are legitimate.

- *Validity* means that the right issues—not "fake" ones—are on the table.
- *Reliability* means that the information on which decisions are based is accurate.

Ground Rules for Effective Decision Making

Communities frequently form decision-making groups to solve problems. In addition, community decision-making groups should adopt ground rules. The principles mentioned in this section will enhance the inclusiveness, trustworthiness, viability, validity, and reliability of the decision-making process.

Respect for People and Ideas

Respect for people is vital. Every person deserves attention and consideration. Group members should listen attentively to every speaker, avoiding negative body language such as scowling, eye-rolling, head-shaking, or other silent but effective means of telling the speaker that he or she is not important. At the same time, speakers and presenters must respect the people who are listening by making points succinctly and avoiding repetition.

Respect people

Part of respecting people is respecting their ideas. However, respect does not mean differences cannot be expressed; respect for ideas implies and requires that those ideas be tested. On the other hand, ideas should not be referred to in scornful terms such as "that's a stupid idea." Even if one particular idea is not strong, it may spark another idea in someone else that becomes a building block for community progress.

Respect ideas

Resist Decision Avoidance Psychosis

Make timely decisions Just as some evidence of losing weight is essential if one is to be motivated to continue a weight-loss program, decision progress is essential for the group to reach its goals. Although progress does not have to occur overnight, the group must periodically come to decisions, advance certain alternatives, forsake other alternatives, and move on. Groups prone to decision avoidance psychosis—that is, groups that delay and delay the making of a decision—will lose the interest, commitment, and participation of their membership.

Honor Time Commitments

Respect time In today's complex life, time is a crucial resource. Time commitments to the meeting process must be honored if commitment to the entire community development process is to be sustained. Meetings must start and end on time. Individuals can plan around them—hiring baby-sitters or making arrangements for coverage at home or work. Dragging out meetings, failing to start on time, or having to meet again to deal with issues that should have been settled at the previous meeting erodes commitment to the larger process. People who are not sure they can depend on the time commitment they have been promised will not attend meetings.

Respect for the Agenda

Respect the agenda Attending a community meeting involves getting information ahead of time, thinking about that information, and preparing to discuss it. Individuals have the right to expect that the energy they have invested in meeting preparation will be honored by focused activity at the meeting. For example, consider how one might feel after going to the movie theater to see a much anticipated—and advertised—movie, only to hear the manager say, "Oh, that didn't get much play, so I sent it back. We're running something else tonight."

Conclusion

Everyone who is involved in community development efforts wants them to be successful. Avoiding the obstacles to effective group process is a key element to working effectively in community development efforts, as is setting up appropriate group structures. The different perspectives of all group members must be melded into workable decision making. Solid procedures and process will not produce that result, but they are an important step toward it. Sloppy procedures almost always create more problems than they solve.

References

Argyris, C. (1985). *Strategy, change, and defensive routines*. Boston: Pitman.

Cohen, M., March, J., & Olson, J. (1972, March). A garbage can model of organizational choice. *Administrative Science Quarterly, 17*, 1–25.

Gamson, W. (1966). Rancorous conflict in community politics. *American Sociological Review, 31*, 71–81.

Harvey, J. (1974, Summer). The Abilene paradox. *Organizational Dynamics*, pp. 63–80.

Hoffer, E. (1951). *The true believer.* New York: Harper.

Janis, I. (1983). *Groupthink: Psychological studies of policy decisions and fiascoes*. Boston: Houghton-Mifflin.

Jones, W. T. (1952). *History of Western philosophy*. New York: Harcourt Brace.

Linz, J. J. (1964). Robert Michels. In D. Sills (Ed.), *International encyclopedia of social sciences* (pp. 265–272). New York: MacMillan.

Michels, R. (1949). *Political parties*. Glencoe, IL: Free Press.

Reisman, D. (1954). *Individualism reconsidered*. Glencoe, IL: Free Press.

Sen, A. (1992). *Inequality reexamined*. Cambridge, MA: Harvard University Press.

Tuchman, B. (1984). *The march of folly*. New York: Knopf.

Chapter 2
Responsibilities of Community Committees

Community decision-making committees have many responsibilities. This chapter details two of those responsibilities in a broad way: member selection and diversity and building trust and empathy. Because chairperson and member responsibilities are important, entire chapters are devoted to them later in this book.

Member Selection

Members of community decision-making groups should be selected with an eye for inclusion; a variety of perspectives must be present. Several principles should guide member selection.

Engage Stakeholders

Although it is not possible to have all stakeholders as members of steering groups or subgroups, having a broad range of them is essential to the community decision-making process. In community service, the types of stakeholders range from consumers to providers and many individuals in the middle. Many cross-community goals such as economic development, health

A range of stakeholders

15

planning, and social planning will have a coordinating or steering group with subgroups working on more specific problems. Even in a service subarea, such as HIV/AIDS concerns, there may be many interests and organizations that need a central place to discuss and work out differences. A steering group will have the broadest cross-section of stakeholders, and work groups will have a more focused stakeholder membership.

Engage Citizens

Citizens In some sense, all citizens can be seen as stakeholders; however, some have perspectives that are broader and different from those of special interests, and these views must be presented during the decision-making process. One community model includes a large committee of citizens and stakeholders that may be subordinate to a steering committee of more focused citizen or stakeholder involvement.

Engage a Range of Ages, Races, and Genders

Diverse membership Because there are many community groups that have a variety of interests, there should be a diversity of membership by age, race, and gender. Single-sex groups or groups of one age range or ethnicity that do not have the broadest scope of membership should be reconstituted with an eye toward broader inclusion.

Engage a Range of Leadership

Leaders and followers A balance should exist among community leadership and community followers. Most communities have influential individuals who often appear in decision-making groups. Their perspective and experience are vital; however, followers must be involved as well, because people who have not historically taken leadership roles have perspectives that may be different and as valuable as those of community leaders.

Diversity Benefits and Problems

Diversity in composition is a positive attribute for decision-making groups. However, problems can arise with respect to the management of diverse groups.

Representation and Representativeness

One problematic aspect of diverse groups is understanding and working out the differences between representation and representativeness. When social workers discuss stakeholder and citizen involvement, a diversity of race and gender, or power bases, they mean representation. *Representation* means having some differences among perspectives and in this sense is used statistically, as of a representative sample.

However, the issue of *representativeness* is approached differently. Individuals invited to join in the community process do not necessarily represent or speak authoritatively for the groups of which they are members. For example, a female group member does not speak for all or even some women. An African American member does not speak for or represent some or all African Americans. Social workers should understand that the views of women, African Americans, and others are views of individuals shaped by their backgrounds and informed by their experiences but not necessarily speaking for their groups. Social workers who want to find out what various community subgroups think should use a survey or assessment of community needs with that subgroup. To turn to a female member and ask, "What do the women think on this issue?" is to seek false data and put the individual in a position of discomfort. At the same time, members must see themselves as individuals and not as spokespeople for women, the African American community, or other groups. Group members should speak for themselves.

Representation versus representativeness

Work Styles

Diversity brings different work styles. Some differences come from group members' jobs or careers. When community volunteers get together, often there is discussion about the differences in time pressure between those who have jobs and those who do not. The former often feel more pressure than the latter. Although most individuals have different amounts of time available at different times of the day, week, and year, the amount of time available should not be confused with the amount of time necessary and agreed on, which should drive the decision-making process. Thus, the group member who is extremely busy should think through commitments and make appropriate arrangements so **Different** that the necessary time is available. Furthermore, the **work styles** group must honor those arrangements and not expand the time commitments required. Individuals who have fewer time constraints must not let the availability of time be a process driver to exclude contributions of other members of the community.

There are other differences. Some people are brisk and businesslike; others approach decision making in a more deliberate manner. Each type of person may arrive at the same point within the same time frame, but each may irritate the other. Adjustments to those differences are needed. Groups may want to try a Meyers–Briggs assay of members to explore some of these differences (see Kiersey & Bates, 1984).

Another difference relates to pressure for final action or openness. Some people are psychologically attuned to seek final action or closure. One approach to this phenomenon is the "Zeigarnik effect," which is the tension to complete a task once it is begun (see Deutch, 1968). For example, this kind of person knows what he or she wants at the supermarket, makes a beeline for that section, buys the product, and leaves the store. Other individuals are more inclined to seek openness. They might know what they want, but as they find it in one supermarket, they wonder whether another supermarket has a better selection and quality and lower price, and they visit three or four supermarkets before making a decision. Each of these personality temperaments tends to annoy individuals with the opposite orientation. Recognition of these differences can soften their effect by bringing differences in style into the open.

Learning Styles

Part of the community development process is learning, and people have different learning styles.

- *Writers.* People who learn by reading written material tend to be oriented to the written word. They find reading the most comfortable medium through which to absorb ideas and concepts.
- *Listeners.* Some people who are more oral than visual in nature may be word oriented but like to hear rather than read the words. For them, a presentation with bulleted lists and summarized concepts is most effective.
- *Visuals.* Some people are visually oriented, but not to words. Instead, they like pictures. For them, graphs, drawings, and other visual summaries are the most effective.
- *The forest versus the trees.* Some people are forest oriented; they like the big picture laid out—with the key concepts mentioned here and there—and they fill in the blanks later. Others cannot grasp the big picture without some sense of the surrounding trees and shrubs; they like to build up to larger decisions. To be most effective, try to give the "forest" person the big picture first. Conversely, give the "tree" person some initial details to work with first.

Different learning styles

Personal and Community Agendas: Partisans and Statespersons

Partisan and statesperson

Everyone has a personal agenda and reasons why he or she became involved in the community process. For example, agencies may feel the need for involvement to protect their own interests; consumers, clients, and customers may feel that their perspectives should be the determining ones. Community volunteer participants have the difficult role of being both partisan and statesperson. The *partisan* pursues his or her own ends; the *statesperson* actively seeks to understand and construct the community view but understands that his or her views might not be well served by a community solution and does not lobby for his or her own perspective. At a minimum, the management of these conflicts involves recognizing up front that there are conflicts.

Several steps can be taken to resolve these issues.

Identify an inclusive decision

- *Seek a community solution.* One view of community process is that these orientations should fight it out, with the strongest winning. That, however, is not the view of most community intervention professionals. Instead, they seek to identify a solution that incorporates elements from all interests, but the solution is not driven by one power. Community professionals seek a win–win rather than a me–win solution.

Articulate the community view

- *Keep vocalizing a community view.* Group management involves self-reflection and the need to continually articulate the importance of a community view and the continual testing of individual proposals in the light of a community view.

Own your view

- *Be candid about your personal views.* Ethical responsibility requires not masking an individual's views as community views. This responsibility involves openness to community influence, even if one ultimately retains his or her own partisan view (which is always an option).

In addition, participation in the community decision-making process requires a willingness to step up to the discussion. For example, if social workers as agency executives are thinking of undertaking a particular action, it might be appropriate and civil to share those intentions with the community group and get feedback and reaction. It is unsettling to return from a community meeting to news that one agency—whose director was sitting at the meeting and said nothing—is taking action that affects other agencies in the group.

The terms of sharing in discussion require an explicit statement of how a particular issue is to be approached. There are three ways that individual members can approach the group to get advice. For example, an agency director may say, "I have a particular point of view; I would like to hear your reaction. I am not offering my point of view from the perspective of my changing it, but I would like to see what you think." This statement is a type 1 statement. **Terms of sharing**

A type 2 statement could be, "As an agency director, I am tending in direction X. I have not made up my mind and welcome your input. However, I make no promises with respect to what I will do with that input." A type 3 statement could be, "As an agency director, I am tending toward direction X. I have not made up my mind nor has our board, and I want to take your wishes into account. Therefore, I am offering to adjust our trajectory toward X once I know what your thinking is. I am not going to ask for your approval of our conclusions from your review; that remains with us. However, I will make certain adjustments and explain to you later at least how I saw those adjustments being made."

Community power

There also are aspects to personal and community agendas that have to do with community power or the lack of it. Sometimes, influential individuals display an irritating sense of entitlement or arrogance. Most often this is not intended, but still it comes across to less powerful and less well-connected people as arrogance. Although it usually is not necessary to remind powerful community leaders that humility is an important virtue, it might not hurt.

Geopolitical Differences

"Where are you from?"

Geopolitical differences involve the geographic places people come from and their differences in prevailing attitudes and orientations. Urban and rural backgrounds are common differences, but there are many variations in urban areas (for example, by ethnic group or neighborhood) and in rural areas (for example, local traditions and resident backgrounds). What people in the city may perceive as a community solution may not be the best solution for people in the country and vice versa. A community view looks at both sets of needs as legitimate and worthy of attention, respects the people and ideas involved in the solutions, and seeks to craft a solution that has appropriate portions addressing the needs of the people in each location.

Building Empathy and Trust

Developing trust

Empathy and trust are essential to the successful community decision-making process. *Empathy* is the sense of proactive understanding, both intellectually and emotionally, of where other people are coming from; it is a sense of "feeling as," for example, if a woman talks about her own and other women's concerns with regard to women's health, other group members must put themselves in her position as far as possible. It is not enough to recognize the viability of that position although that is an important first step. A sense of active sympathy—a sense of "feeling for"—also is needed. For example, "I understand (I think, I hope) where you are coming from on these issues, and I can try to feel as you might feel."

Trust (as previously defined) must exist in the community decision-making procedures.

Trust in Procedure

Once trust is established, integrity must follow. *Trust in procedure* means that things are going to go as they have been announced. For example, time commitments will be honored and agendas will be followed.

Trust in procedure

Trust in Process

Trust in process means that "what one sees is what one gets." People must believe the meeting they attend is the real meeting. When backroom activity—secret meetings of some members and powerful agenda makers who often never attend an open meeting—goes on, the community development process is not authentic.

Trust in process

Trust in People

Trust in people means that group members must be able to share their views and feelings without being ridiculed and insulted, without being approached in a sarcastic manner, and without being interrupted. The entire group must see that these norms are maintained. Trust should also extend outside of the meeting room. As the decision-making process proceeds, possibilities may arise that require confidentiality issues to be explored, especially if ideas are preliminary and decisions have not been made. As individuals share exploratory ideas, they need to feel comfortable that others will respect the preliminary nature of the discussions. Members do not want to

Trust in people

receive a telephone call after the meeting from some community person who is not a part of the process saying, "I understand this is going to happen, and here's what I think." Inappropriate sharing outside the group leads to the development of destructive norms that affect vital processes and causes members not to attend meetings at all.

It is also important that group members not take advantage of the process to advance their interests by using "inside information" gained from the group. For example, it is unethical for a wealthy group participant who hears about a business opportunity to use that information and quickly make a personal profit from it.

Conclusion

As individuals enter the community decision-making process, pressures and differences surface. All group participants need to keep these differences in mind and avoid letting them become disruptive to the process of community development.

References

Deutch, M. (1968). Field theory. In D. Sills (Ed.), *International encyclopedia of the social sciences* (Vol. 5, pp. 406–417). New York: Free Press.

Kiersey, D., & Bates, M. (1984). *Please understand me* (4th ed.). Del Mar, CA: Prometheus Nemesis.

Chapter 3
The Group Chairperson

B eing a group chairperson is a complicated and problematic job that involves balancing and interchanging positions and roles. Part of the problem many chairpersons face is that they do not know what to do as chairperson.

A chairperson is an executive leader. The executive part involves the position and what is needed, such as running the meetings and making sure that solutions decided in the meetings are implemented. The leadership part involves taking leadership and accepting followership, requires being out front and hanging back, and embraces risk taking while letting others take risks as well. This chapter helps address the uncertainty that surrounds both levels of tasks.

Executive Responsibilities

From Virtuoso to Maestro

The chairperson-designate may have interests to advance and positions to articulate. In that respect, the chairperson-to-be is like a virtuoso violinist who becomes the conductor. When the chairperson position is assumed, a broader, more diplomatic, community-based view must be taken. Much like the violinist who

Becoming the conductor

becomes the conductor, the member who becomes the chairperson must leave most of his or her partisan interests behind.

Asking Questions

Using the "question technique"

The chairperson receives added authority from the group members, and thus his or her statements carry more weight. As a result, the chairperson who is accustomed to expressing her or his views must assume a quieter role. Statements and contributions should be modulated and phrased more tentatively. Often the best way to approach a topic is through questions. Asking questions such as, "What are the implications of this approach?" or "How can we improve this proposal?" will guide the group better than statements. Statements cut off comment and invite rebuttal; questions invite thought and response.

Following Procedure

Keeping the rules

Each group should establish some procedures for its meetings. Once established, it is the chairperson's responsibility to see that those procedures are fulfilled. The chairperson must be prepared for meetings, have and follow the agenda, and follow up on agreements. If the chairperson fulfills his or her responsibilities, then other group members can be expected to follow as well.

Managing Difficult People

Saying "wrap it up, please"

Chairpersons have to deal with difficult people. For example, when speakers drone on, and chairperson will need to say, "Please wrap up your comments in the interest of time." For the more problematic person—say, someone who is hostile toward others—the chairperson may need to meet with the individual outside the meeting (Bramson, 1981) and privately explore issues and convey the effect (negative in this case) that his or her behavior is having on the community group.

Although there are individuals who are hard to deal with, many of the problems with difficult people can be attributed to lack of process or sloppy meetings that do not address issues and convey a sense of wasted time to participants. No wonder that people become difficult. Developing fair, balanced procedures that generate accomplishment and create norms that can be enforced by the group are important.

Working with Staff or Facilitator

Community decision-making groups often have a community facilitator to assist the group with its activities. The facilitator receives direction from the chairperson. Roles of staff members must also be worked out with the chairperson. Once roles have been established, the chairperson should avoid changing them to ensure continuity. The chairperson must find time to work out a set of meeting strategies and tactics with staff and facilitator.

Working with the facilitator

Once the meeting strategies have been worked out and an agenda crafted, it is the chairperson's responsibility to follow the strategies and agenda, unless something unexpected comes up. If unanticipated events occur frequently, there probably is inadequate planning before the meetings.

Making Key Contributions in Meetings

The following four types of contributions are especially important. The chairperson chooses which areas in which to make contributions depending on what the group needs.

Intellectual Contributions

The chairperson makes intellectual contributions including suggesting ideas, suggesting modifications of

Suggesting ideas

the ideas of others, and blending the ideas of people in the group into a single, coherent idea. This role is assumed if needed and not because the chairperson is good at it. If plenty of good ideas are being suggested, the chairperson should wait until his or her input is needed.

Interpersonal Contributions

Supporting people

Interpersonal contributions involve praising people who have made good contributions, seeing that everyone has a chance to contribute (enhancing the underparticipator), and cooling down someone who is participating too much (tempering the overparticipator). Doing interpersonal work means doing all those big and little things that help the process move smoothly. Again, the chairperson should do them only when and if needed.

Task Contributions

Keeping on track

Every community group and its subgroups have tasks that are essential to complete. The chairperson supports the setting and construction of time lines to complete tasks. Time lines provide structure to achieve the group's goals. Some techniques, such as Gantt and program, evaluation, and review technique (PERT) charts, can help develop time lines (see Childress, 1995, for more information).

Process Contributions

Keeping everyone involved

The chairperson should be sensitive to the pace of community process, that is, the way a community "does its business." Tasks must be accomplished, but participation is vital as well. Decisions that are made need community support. Chairpersons should establish a tone and a pace that are comfortable for the community in which they are working.

Leadership Responsibilities

An individual can be appointed to a position but cannot be appointed leader—he or she has to step into that position. Leadership involves taking new steps and thinking about new ideas and approaches. Effective leadership involves convincing others that they can comfortably follow the leader. Experienced leaders understand that leadership involves risk taking, voicing the difficult problem, and setting the strategic mission.

Leading

Leadership creates followership, a relationship that can be called the "leadership exchange." Leadership exchange occurs when the leader risks himself or herself to establish future directions for the group. The new directions address knotty problems in ways that the group recognizes have potential to solve those problems and help the community, and the group rewards the leader with cooperation.

Leadership exchange

A leader does not advance his or her own agenda. Leadership involves creating new possibilities and inviting others to contribute. Leadership involves innovation and selflessness. Leadership helps groups make changes in their community.

Creating the future

There are two aspects to leadership—the first is outlining a possible future and the second is helping create the conditions and excitement that encourage people to contribute. Because the group members are the ones who have to make the decisions, it is crucial that the members contribute ideas and support. Effective leaders develop an overall vision from parts of ideas of themselves and others, making solutions to problems a group process.

Outlining a future and encouraging contributions

The chairperson must distribute the role of leadership among the members of the steering and work groups and into the community. The *empowerment principle*, a conviction that says that the membership in the committee process expands a member's ability to be a leader and take leadership roles, is sought here.

Ability to create change without crisis

Leadership is about change. A leader has to be able to change and help others to change. "Leadership is the ability to create change without crisis" (personal communication with R. Quinn, professor, Business School, University of Michigan, May 13, 1996).

Building Capacity in Others

Helping others be strong

Leadership should pass from person to person—from the chairperson to group member—as the decision-making process progresses. Chairpersons should encourage others to take leadership roles. Leadership has a fluid quality. Groups where everyone has a role but everyone also helps everyone else are good metaphors for the meeting process. In effective groups, everybody takes leadership, and multiple leaders are a dynamic aspect of leadership. Leadership is like a jazz orchestra; everyone has a chance—should have a chance—to be featured.

Followership

Following as needed

Followership is essential so that others can lead, and the best meetings, workplaces, or families are those in which everyone has a chance both to lead and to follow. If one individual is always leading, others must always follow, and thus a routine emerges. Followership involves letting someone else move into the leadership role, both structurally ("At the upcoming meeting will you 'take the lead' on discussing this issue?") and procedurally ("I know that you have a lot of knowledge about this area. Could you get us going?").

Because it is difficult to exercise leadership in every area and on every issue, leaders need the support of followers, and few things are more discouraging to a potential leader than finding that there are no followers. Effective leadership is balanced with effective followership.

Conclusion

The chairperson is like a conductor of an orchestra. Although chairpersons are vital to the process of community decision making, like the work of the conductor, they often get work done through others. The chairperson has a challenge that can be met more easily if good working relations are established with staff and facilitators, contributions by others are encouraged, and leadership is balanced with effective followership.

References

Bramson, R. M. (1981). *Coping with difficult people*. New York: Ballantine Books.

Childress, B. (1995). Program evaluation and review technique. In J. Maurer, J. Shueman, M. Rowe, & R. Bechener (Eds.), *The encyclopedia of business* (pp. 1201–1203). Detroit: Gale Research.

Chapter 4
The Community Group Member

G roup members often believe that there is nothing to learn about being a member. Members
show up and doze off until the meeting is over (unfortunately, this attitude is all-too prevalent). However,
members have responsibilities, and their active participation is critical to the success of the community group.

Member Responsibilities

Group members have many responsibilities; however,
most have not had instruction in fulfilling them.

Being Prepared

**Being
prepared** Members have a responsibility to review and think
about meeting material in advance. Organizers work
hard to prepare advance material for meetings, and
members who come unprepared are not making an
appropriate effort.

Aiding the Chairperson

**Helping the
chairperson** Most people feel that it is the chairperson's responsibility to keep order in the meeting. If a member acts
inappropriately, other members may complain later
that the chairperson did not exercise proper authority
or discipline. Keeping order, however, is everyone's

responsibility. The chairperson cannot exercise discipline all the time. If that happens, a student–teacher relationship emerges, with the chairperson–teacher being the custodian of order and the member–student taking no responsibility for discipline.

Group members should come to the aid of the chairperson. Members do not have to wait for the chairperson to express control before helping out. Consider a member who has been attacking another member's proposal for several minutes. A community group member might say, "I think you're being a little hard on this proposal, and you're making people feel bad about it. It has some problems; I see one or two myself, but I think we owe it to everyone to have a balanced discussion." The individual is held in check, but the chairperson did not have to exercise disciplinary measures because a member of the group did. Group members do not perform that duty often, but it is effective when they do. The chairperson will appreciate some help.

The scenario may be reversed. For example, the chairperson makes the same comment. At that point, the chairperson would appreciate a member saying, "Yes, I agree with that, and perhaps we could focus on some of the positives as well as the negatives."

Modulating Participation

Some meetings have high levels of participation, with everyone contributing; other meetings have less participation. Members should balance their behavior with the typical behavior in the meeting. For example, enthusiastic members should try to hold back in meetings where the culture and style are more subdued.

Watching your level of participation

Reasons exist to adjust one's self-presentation, because everyone notices how much someone participates and adjusts their view of his or her credibility as a result.

Don't be an overparticipator The overparticipator is recognized as someone who does not give others a chance. Even though his or her ideas may be good, a member who overparticipates against group-established norms risks lowering his or her effectiveness.

But don't just keep quiet A member who does not participate at all may be thought of as being critical and hostile, even if this is not true. Although it may be appropriate not to say anything, other members may think the silent member is quietly criticizing them. When members who are speaking do not know what other people are thinking, they tend to assume that the silent member is thinking about them disapprovingly. Some individuals may imagine that the silent member dislikes them. Thus, other members act toward the silent member as if he or she is hostile. This reaction is frequently a surprise to the silent member. The best course for a member who does not want to participate in a meeting is to make a comment to that effect.

Not Dumping Problems on the Group

Helping the group help you Many members feel that if they do not like a proposal it is enough to say, "I don't like that." However, stating only the negative is insufficient; something more assertive is needed. "Dumping problems on the group" refers to the practice of expressing one's feelings and then expecting the group to find the answer to a question, for example, "If John doesn't like this mileage proposal, what would he like?"

This question—"What would he like?"—suggests an answer. A group member should suggest a solution when pointing out problems with a proposal, for example, "I really don't like this mileage proposal, because I feel there is not enough money to make it worthwhile for me to use my own car. Twenty cents per mile is well below what others provide. However—and this may not be possible—but at 27 cents a mile I would find myself in support." This contribution focuses the discussion on an alternative proposal rather than inviting the group to say, "How about 21 cents?" or "How about 22 or 23 cents?" In the example, the speaker recognized that the proposed higher amount might not be okay; however, the proposal provided a focus for the discussion to move toward a goal.

Providing Support for Other Members

Group membership requires attention to the other members and their interests and needs. Members have an obligation to provide support for other members, for example, reining in someone because he or she was too harsh on another member's proposal. Positive comments of support and appreciation are always welcome but infrequently offered.

Supporting others

Members should listen to and validate the ideas of others, especially when new ideas are discussed. New ideas are risky because, although they are needed and wanted most, at the same time they are threatening (new ideas usually mean doing things differently) and vulnerable (they usually are incomplete). Often these two features—threat and vulnerability—create a frenzy in community groups, during which everybody jumps on the bandwagon against the new idea.

New ideas are most vulnerable and in need of support

Conclusion

Being a member of a community group carries responsibilities. Members need to be prepared, proactive, supportive, and engaging. Group members should think of themselves as part of a community team and realize that the team's performance determines success.

Chapter 5
The Community Facilitator

Community decision-making groups often have a facilitator or community organizer who helps them do their work. The community facilitator has many frequently linked roles. Generally, he or she works on behalf of the action-planning organization to facilitate its activities and to provide information and service to decision-making groups. Because most groups do not meet all the time, someone must prepare correspondence, keep files, and do research. When the group is not in session, a facilitator pulls together information about relevant issues, obtains comparative information, and makes sure that all information is properly assembled.

The process of community facilitation is sometimes called the "staffing function." The word "staff" has two meanings. As a noun, it refers to an employee of an organization. This usage refers to line authority and reflects the hierarchy of the organization. As a verb it refers to the process of providing a specific service to a committee or board. This usage implies services and comes from the "staff" part of the staff–line distinction (Simon, Thompson, & Smithburg, 1956/1991). In the staff–line distinction, staff stand off to one side and have no line (decision-making) authority. Such authority they do have comes from knowledge, expertise, or proximity to the decision-making positions in the line organization. The community facilitator or "staffer" does not have line authority.

Given this distinction, the most important tasks of the facilitator are

- coordinator–manager
- aide to the chairperson
- researcher and knowledge synthesizer
- writer–documentor
- aide to consultants
- consultant and professional expert.

Although each role requires different skills and competencies, all are essential to the optimal functioning of a community group. Although this chapter is geared toward the professional facilitator, the information about expectations and tasks also can be helpful to volunteers.

Coordinator–Manager

A community facilitator is involved in many activities as a coordinator–manager. Sometimes the problems of mechanics at a meeting overshadow the substantive purpose, and problems such as lack of parking, reimbursement concerns, and inadequate meeting rooms consume so much time that work cannot go on. The community facilitator's responsibility is to avoid these situations through planning and action before the meeting.

Coordinating and managing

Although there are unique situations, in general planning problems come from lack of attention to common themes and needs. Thus, the role of the coordinator–manager is not trivial, and the mechanics of preparation are critical. Once planning is under control, attention can move toward the preparation of meeting materials (see chapter 7).

Frequently, the facilitator helps the chairperson prepare for meetings. In addition, in the course of his or her job, the facilitator learns a great deal of substantive information that he or she passes along to the chairperson or group.

Aide to the Chairperson

Helping the chairperson

The community facilitator's tasks involve elements of leadership and followership. The facilitator usually has an assignment to one or more committees or work groups, and the chairperson, within the limits of agency policy and procedure, is his or her boss. Through that relationship, many of the facilitator's ideas and orientations become expressed, and through working with and aiding the chairperson, the facilitator develops an influence on the committee. In this manner, the professional skill of the community facilitator is manifest.

Following the chairperson

Community facilitators who perform well in other roles often fail in this one because they do not develop a good working relationship with the chairperson. Mechanics—doing the work of preparation—and dynamics—establishing good interpersonal connections—are involved in establishing this good working relationship.

There often are many different orientations to the policy problem under consideration. Although the community facilitator may have his or her own perspective, the facilitator's perspective is subordinate to those of the chairperson and the committee. While writing policy, a clear distinction should be made between the opinions of the group and the recommendations of the facilitator. If an orientation can be established from the beginning that recognizes the integrity and the predominance of the chairperson, the committee will make progress.

This orientation might be viewed as staff abrogation of responsibility rather than the proper filling of that responsibility. The community facilitator is a professional, often trained in a distinct field. Training, professional status, and background give the facilitator special responsibilities for developing her or his view, but the facilitator is only a knowledgeable servant of the committee and the chairperson. The facilitator must act ethically and let the committee and chairperson act in the capacities for which they have been appointed and help them make the appropriate decisions.

However, the community facilitator has an opportunity to express his or her views to the chairperson in private. The facilitator should initiate such discussions early to learn the policy orientation of the chairperson on particular topics. Such discussions continue through the range of topics of the facilitator–chairperson relationship and should ensure that no surprises occur with respect to the facilitator's understanding of the chairperson's positions.

A community facilitator–chairperson conference should be part of the procedures between all facilitators and chairpersons. A conference can take place after agenda items have been determined and the facilitator is preparing a preliminary agenda for review and approval by the chairperson. After this, the discussion (for example, what is the order of agenda items, what are people likely to do at this meeting, what are other problems, and so forth) should turn to elements of meeting planning. Often, the facilitator and chairperson ignore this crucial conference, and the pair have to improvise after the meeting begins. Regular, informal meetings between facilitator and chairperson are the basis for a positive working relationship.

Facilitator–chairperson conference

Other actions occur in these meetings. The community facilitator briefs the chairperson on upcoming issues and concerns and shares intelligence reports. The facilitator should determine if the chairperson needs additional information so the information can be gathered in time for the meeting. Together, the facilitator and chairperson consider meeting strategy and tactics and share feelings and perspectives. There is a good reason for sharing this information at this time, beyond its helpful role in understanding the dynamics of issues. The facilitator plays a relatively neutral role during the meeting; he or she takes minutes and does not participate emotionally in the process. The chairperson, in seeking to convey a statesmanlike posture, also participates in a neutral way, seeking to temper the hotheaded and fire up the lukewarm. Therefore, prior ventilation of feelings is proper preparation for remaining effectively neutral during the meeting. Thus, the informal meeting session is crucial to meeting preparation.

Researcher and Knowledge Synthesizer

Gathering and blending knowledge The community facilitator is responsible for securing knowledge and presenting it to the committee in a form that can be used for decision-making purposes. The facilitator should not approach research in a scholarly or scientific mode in which much time is used and in-depth surveys of the literature are undertaken. Procedures need to be developed for doing quick but thorough literature reviews and for delivering state-of-the-art briefings. The facilitator may want to use a meta-analysis, which involves reviewing all recent studies on a topic and determining what the evidence says from such a review.

The community facilitator is a knowledge synthesizer and communicator rather than a knowledge developer. The contributions he or she makes to knowledge come from developing fresh information—finding
new categories through which information can be gathered and pulling together split or fragmented information. This part of the job is theoretical or concep-
tual, but it is here that the community facilitator can
affect the thinking of the committee. A key element in
managing ideas is to *have* ideas, and the ability to come
up with new ideas or to present old ideas with new
twists that make them useful is an important skill. To
do this, the facilitator needs to gather information.

Information Gathering

Information can come from several sources.

Staff Sources

Some information is already in the possession of the
community facilitator, because he or she usually has
some substantive area of competence, such as criminal
justice, social planning, child welfare, or community
organization.

*Libraries, Data Banks, and Compilations
of Abstracts and Dissertations*

The standard academic sources of information—libraries, data banks, and compilations of abstracts and dissertations—should be checked first. However, the community facilitator must go beyond this checking to develop
personal resources that augment his or her ability to obtain information quickly. Facilitators should get to know
reference librarians. Most individuals do not know enough
about libraries, and the reference librarian can find information quickly. It is sometimes appropriate to hire a librarian to do an initial search and assemble copies of relevant material for the facilitator to review. Much time is

**Gathering
information**

**Current
expertise**

Library sources

wasted looking for material that could be gathered more efficiently by someone who is more familiar with the information sources.

Computer-based Sources

Computer sources The community facilitator can make arrangements to use computer-based search facilities that are available through most universities. Such facilities vary in their complexity, but generally an individual formulates a computer-based search using indexes of key terms. The indexes allow searches of many large databases. A quick scan of a search can provide a number of titles. A better-refined search will find abstracts of articles that can be printed and mailed or, if the database is on site, made immediately available to the searcher. This process shortens the search and allows the facilitator to spend time synthesizing instead of collecting information. A discussion of searching the library and computer-based sources, including the Internet and the World Wide Web, is in appendix 1, which includes community-oriented Web sites and instructions on how to use the Internet.

Knowledgeable Individuals

Relationship sources The community facilitator should know key knowledgeable individuals to call to get their perspectives on the issues under consideration, for example, lawyers are essential when legal questions arise. This technique is usually effective for locating the main points of a developing line of thought; more conventional research can provide additional answers.

Networking is one kind of relationship-sourcing. A facilitator typically has both professional and community-based individuals in his or her network with whom to talk and obtain information.

News Media and Professional Publications
Community facilitators should read at least one national and one local newspaper daily and subscribe to
professional publications. Community members expect
that the facilitator will be knowledgeable about current events; he or she is expected to be the eyes and
ears of the committee and do the reading and listening
that members cannot do. The facilitator should be proactive with information and bring it to the attention of
the committee. An item here or a conference announcement there should attract the attention of the facilitator as it relates to the task at hand, and he or she should
bring it to the attention of the chairperson. However,
the popular press should be approached cautiously as a
source of technical information; in many cases when
research is reported by the press, important qualifica-
tions slip away from the initial report of the story or
do not catch the reporter's attention.

Daily life sources

Political Considerations
The community facilitator should remember that data
have emotional as well as rational dimensions. Simple
factual reports may create problems for committee
members. For example, reporting on the average
weight of the members of the community and discussing weight as a health risk may trouble some committee members who are struggling with weight-control
problems. Issues about teenage parenting may cause a
reaction from a group member whose teenager is a
parent. Discussion of the broken family index may be
difficult for a committee member who is divorced.
Other types of considerations include the following.

Information generates feelings and conflicts

Minority Interests
The community facilitator should determine if there
are any special minority interests in a policy under

Minority interests

consideration and what information would be helpful to them.

Committee–Boss Constituency

Committee–boss constituency
The community facilitator should be aware of any implications a policy proposal has for the constituencies of any members of the committee. In addition, implications should be determined for the boss or executive of the agency that hires the facilitator, if that agency is not the committee itself. Being able to assess such effects in advance allows the affected parties to take early action.

Uninvolved Groups

Uninvolved groups
The community facilitator should give thought to groups or individuals who have been left out of the decision-making process because no one initially thought of asking them to participate or considered their needs. This omission is serious because there is a lack of input from the group left out, because the solution will not be all inclusive, and because the slighted group may oppose the solution out of anger.

Political–Scientific Conflicts

Political–scientific conflicts
Political–scientific conflicts occur when science and popular will clash. For example, a discussion of the importance of fathers in the family and the dangers to children in families without fathers may cause conflicts with lesbian households where an adoption or artificial insemination has occurred or with members of a subcommunity with a large number of single-mother families.

Personal Issues

Personal issues
Individuals have personal sensitivities and concerns. For example, female, Jewish, or African American members usually dislike being asked, "Well, what do women, Jews, Blacks, etc., think about this issue. . . ." The

community facilitator needs to be culturally and personally sensitive to these issues.

Writer–Documentor

The role of the writer–documentor is an extension of the role of knowledge synthesizer, but this role stresses formal exchange of information. The knowledge the community facilitator pulls together is generally given to the committee in writing as background information for its work. The facilitator is usually responsible for writing most proposals that go before the committee. This aspect of the job is among the most frustrating because of the labor-intensive nature of writing and rewriting the material. In addition, the facilitator usually takes the meeting minutes, and these have special importance to the committee's work.

Exchanging information

KNOWER System

Community facilitators can use the KNOWER system for writing drafts and documents for community groups (Tropman, 1984). The name is an acronym using the following terms:

KNOWER system

- **kn**owledge
- **o**rganization in the form of an outline that is approved by the chairperson, consultants, and other relevant individuals
- **w**riting the draft
- **e**valuation of the initial product through reactions from others
- **r**ewriting the draft, often several times.

Writing is one key aspect of the facilitator's job, and many community group members and organizers do not know what community workers think until they see it on paper. Writing also can reveal sloppy thinking and encourage revision and refinement of the thought process.

It is important for the community facilitator to keep a balanced perspective when writing. A written document provides the opportunity to introduce the facilitator's bias into the content. The facilitator should resist this temptation, because his or her influence must be given in more open ways rather than through subtle changes in the text. If the committee believes that the facilitator cannot be trusted, his or her influence with the committee erodes.

The facilitator should rewrite draft information to avoid the process of group editing. Once a group reads a written draft, the urge to edit or rewrite is almost overwhelming. If rewriting drafts is a problem for the facilitator, group editing will be especially troublesome. A good technique is to ask members for comments, put these on the draft, and review and make appropriate changes to the document after the meeting. The facilitator can blend the various comments into improvements.

Types of Written Documents

Kinds of documents   Technical reports, policy drafts, and meeting minutes are the three main types of written materials the community facilitator manages.

Technical Reports

Technical reports   Assembling scientific and technical material that the committee will consider is the most complicated writing for the facilitator. For this material to be meaningful and useful, it must be more than a recitation of what others have said; the technical report must be a synthesis of common elements, a balance of various points of view, and an attempt to show where the weight of evidence lies.

Most material used by the community facilitator in working up policy materials for consideration will not be known to committee members. Care must be taken to provide correct reporting as well as accurate reflection of the differences that exist in the material. The facilitator should keep copies of all materials in a file and when the syntheses are prepared make references (or footnotes) to specific sources and quotes so they may be checked later for accuracy and to ensure that reference material is available when decisions are made.

Policy Drafts
Committee members have a high interest in policy **Policy drafts** drafts, usually reading every word. For the draft, the facilitator should begin with the main issue, and then, while still on the first page, add the proposed or revised text during the meeting. If the text is long, the facilitator can ask to have copies back with notations and harmonize the various suggestions later.

> Policy text needs to be set off in some way, like this, so that readers can see clearly what is proposed.
>
> If the text is a revision, the words that are to be removed are indicated by ~~strikethrough~~ and *new text by italics.*

The facilitator should be aware of his or her psychological reaction to the review that follows. The facilitator's feelings may be hurt if the committee ignores reports; however, too much attention is likely to generate the feeling of nit-picking. Overattention, however, is preferable to underattention.

Because the policy document will represent the committee to the public, members will examine it in detail. However, even the most experienced facilitator cannot anticipate all the nuances of words and the implications these may have for people from different backgrounds and areas of expertise. Therefore, careful review should be expected both psychologically and procedurally (one system—the three-step—is suggested in the section on "Managing the Decision Rules" in chapter 9). Such review means many revisions; five or six are typical. If the facilitator is aware this process is likely to occur, he or she can be prepared to work within it.

Meeting Minutes

Meeting minutes Meeting minutes often are a source of difficulty. Although there is no standard form for writing minutes, some guidelines do exist.

Process minutes, in which the community facilitator tries to record the process of the meeting like a tape recorder, is a poor way to take minutes. The central purpose and content of the meeting can become buried under a wave of process.

Using a "content minutes" approach Content minutes are a solution to this problem. In such minutes, the headings, attendance record, date, and other points (see later discussion) remain the same; however, after that the minutes follow a specific form.

- *Agenda connect.* Along the side of the paper are headings that correspond to agenda topics. Thus, the reader can easily follow the agenda right into the minutes.
- *Summative reflection.* Content minutes aim to capture the main points of the discussion for the reader; no names are used.
- *Decision.* The main decision is recorded.

> *The decision is usually recorded in special type and put in a box. Names, dates, and assignments appear here.*

Well-prepared minutes provide a model of focused discussion; they highlight decisions and provide a means to check and determine what needs to be done, by whom, and when. The essence of the arguments made in the meeting are recorded. Some skill is necessary in judging, evaluating, and fairly reporting different points of view. For this reason, the community facilitator is the most appropriate individual to take minutes. If there is no facilitator, minutes can be taken by group members on a rotating basis.

The message that the minutes give to the members is more important than the simple record-keeping function. Time is wasted in meetings going over old minutes and correcting them; this time can be saved if the facilitator takes precise, economical minutes that do not invite endless recapitulation.

Minutes provide a record of who participated in the decision. For this reason, a list of those present and absent is important. The list provides information about who was involved in the particular decision, information that often is crucial later. Names are listed in alphabetical order, with the chairperson designated as such (in parentheses) after his or her name. This convention is far more important than might be suspected. A departure from alphabetical order is read by members as an order of status, even if that is not intended. It can be devastating to those who find their names at the bottom of the list. The community facilitator lists himself or herself on a separate line, emphasizing the distinction between the facilitator and the members.

It is almost impossible to take good minutes while participating fully in a meeting, and for this reason the community facilitator should temper his or her participation in meetings. The role of the facilitator should be that of participant–observer and is related to the taking of minutes and the need to observe and listen carefully to what is going on. The process is important both for recording the minutes and understanding committee dynamics.

While participating in the meeting, the community facilitator responds to questions and provides clarifications to material for which he or she is responsible. The role of minute taker can be used to help clarify the discussion through the guise of clarifying the minutes. If the facilitator thinks that a decision is not clear, he or she can ask permission to read back what he or she understands the decision to be. The group members can provide clarification.

Aide to Consultants

Helping consultants Community decision-making groups sometimes have the assistance of consultants, both for substantive issues (for example, economic development) and process or technical issues (for example, conflict management). These individuals could be from a nearby university or local talent bank.

Involving consultants requires skill and balance. If the consultants remain too far from the process, they become unhelpful. If they become too close, they become overinvolved and may dominate the process. The community facilitator has an important responsibility in managing or orchestrating consultants, both in person and by providing them information.

The community facilitator needs to know the consultants and their capabilities. The facilitator should seek, with the help of the chairperson, to create a flow of information and assistance to and from the consultants. Sometimes consultants assist the facilitator directly, discussing ideas and reviewing drafts and other written materials. Consultants also can attend meetings to provide technical support and prepare written documents. All activities of consultants should be organized through the facilitator.

Consultant and Professional Expert

The community facilitator has professional expertise and is expected to share it; therefore, sometimes the facilitator is the consultant. Such sharing must be done within the context of the knowledgeable-servant approach, so decision making remains at the community level. Key skills to act as a consultant include

Sharing expertise

- listening actively
- responding empathetically and sympathetically
- giving corrective and supportive feedback
- challenging ideas tactfully but forcefully
- crafting problem-solving rather than fault-finding conversation
- suggesting stimulating, innovative approaches.

See Egan (1994) and Barcus and Wilkinson (1995) for additional advice.

Working the Meeting

Regardless of preparation, much of what happens in community decision-making groups occurs in meetings. Experience and good judgment about participation are crucial. The seen-but-not-heard rule is good to follow for the beginning community facilitator, because it is better to err by being too quiet than by overparticipating. It is much easier to participate more

Helping the meeting move forward

than to trim the level of participation once a pattern of meeting involvement has been established.

Within the meeting itself, the community facilitator can play a role of modest, technical participation, always being careful not to undermine the chairperson. The facilitator can elaborate on reports, offer factual comments, and seek clarification of the comments of others with regard to facts. He or she can offer to obtain additional information on sensitive points. Such an offer made in a strategic, timely fashion could serve to diffuse an inflammatory situation.

The community facilitator plays the role of supportive expert. Sometimes in meetings the facilitator must support ideas that have been developed, add technical validation where important, and head off potential conflicts. For problematic issues, for example, a member states something that is technically wrong, it is best to approach that person at a break. Only under extreme circumstances, for example, if the technical error becomes the basis for action, should the facilitator correct someone publicly.

Working behind the Scenes

Working both sides of the street

In addition to meeting participation, much of what the community facilitator does is behind the scenes, although not under the table. The facilitator has both task and process goals such as helping the community achieve action aims and helping the community become more cohesive. The facilitator sometimes works both sides of the street to provide this help. On one hand, he or she encourages task computation; on the other hand, he or she supports appropriate process. Usually the facilitator does whatever is *not* being done. Thus, if the community group is too task focused the facilitator reminds them of process; if too much process is going on, the facilitator stresses task goals.

However, problems can arise in this process if the facilitator does not know the community well. Egan (1994) discussed potential "minefields"; although his focus is on organizations, his points can apply to communities as well.

- *Covert culture.* Communities have values, beliefs, and attitudes that affect the way members see the world, think about things, and explain events. The facilitator must learn about this culture by spending time getting to know the community.
- *Social system.* Communities have patterns of behavior as well as patterns of culture. Such behavior often represents a combination of public and hidden ways that things are done. The facilitator needs to know the community's locally based patterns.
- *Idiosyncrasies of individuals.* Individuals can be difficult (Bramson, 1981) or just powerful or unique people. The facilitator needs to spend time in the community to get a flavor of who is influential. Once opinion leaders have been identified, the facilitator should spend personal time with them, if possible.
- *Community politics.* Politics is about who does what for whom—about gains and losses, money, power, prestige, and access to jobs. These things are always present in a community. The facilitator needs to know the lay of the political land and be prepared for selfishness, self-centeredness, and greed, helping partisans to become community citizens. The facilitator should prepare himself or herself for loss while working for gain.

Conclusion

The professional community facilitator has many important tasks, and each has unique features. The facilitator's success will be enhanced if she or he learns how to do each of these jobs well. Greater group success can be achieved if the members also are aware of these jobs. Sometimes the facilitator has to educate volunteers about the range and limitations of his or her particular tasks; therefore, the facilitator must be thoroughly knowledgeable about the dimensions of his or her positions and roles.

References

Barcus, J., & Wilkinson, J. (1995). *Handbook of management consulting services*. New York: McGraw-Hill.

Bramson, R. M. (1981). *Working with difficult people*. New York: Ballantine Books.

Egan, G. (1994). *Working the shadow side*. San Francisco: Jossey-Bass.

Simon, H., Thompson, V., & Smithburg, D. (1991). *Public administration*. New Brunswick, NJ: Transaction Publications. Originally published in 1956

Tropman, J. E. (1984). *Policy management in the human services*. New York: Columbia University Press.

Part 2
Conducting Effective Community Group Meetings

Associations of community members do their work in community meetings, and every day numerous meetings address America's social concerns. People discuss and decide what they would like to see in the future of their community. Often, these meetings do not go well. In one of our country's great paradoxes, our emphasis on associations has not been matched with a broadly accepted, constantly improving technology for effective work in groups. The meeting, which is the central mechanism for decision and discussion, is among the most poorly guided of social institutions. It is almost as if there is a bizarre inversion—the more we depend on meetings, the less we know about how to manage them well.

The supposed ineptitude of boards and committees are contained in dozens of humorous asides, such as "a **Meetings often go badly** camel is a horse assembled by a committee," "a board is a group that takes minutes to waste hours," or "a board member is synonymous with dead wood." Consider the following wall poster suggested by Kristoff (1996):

MEETING TO DECIDE
THE RIGHT TIME TO SCHEDULE
THE MEETING TO DECIDE

Partly because of our individualistic society, group efforts are hard to manage in the United States. People frequently use comments such as, "I didn't get any work done; I had to spend the entire day in meetings." This phrase tells a lot about the assumptions of where work is done (alone in our offices) and the extent to which group activities (meetings) interfere with rather than become central to work.

But people do really good work in meetings

No matter how good one's intentions, community development success will remain elusive unless individuals in the community meet, process information, and come up with decisions. How should such a process look, and do we know anything about how to do it? Research done at the University of Michigan (sponsored in part by the 3M Meeting Management Institute) provides some guidance (Tropman, 1996). Participant observation was made

Meeting masters

of meeting masters—individuals in communities in Michigan and across Canada and the United States—who have the reputation for running excellent meetings. Many of these individuals were from community and citizens committees. Others were from government, human services organizations, and corporations.

Excellence has a definition in this context. Meeting masters ran successful meetings that had three elements:

1. Decisions get made.
2. The decisions are of high quality.
3. Participants enjoy themselves.

Almost anyone can run meetings and committees and meet these three criteria for success.

Making the most of the opportunity for group leadership means doing good work in meetings. This section provides community workers with the technology and techniques to make this happen. Chapter 6 focuses on the perspectives the meeting masters had about community meetings. Chapter 7 attends to the process of community meetings. Chapter 8 deals with the skills of guiding community group discussion. Chapter 9 provides help in moving community groups to decisions. Chapter 10 provides some suggestions in structuring evaluation—has the group achieved anything and, if so, is it any good?

References

Kristoff, N. D. (1996, January 20). The land of laureates: Japan's passion for poetry. *New York Times*, p. 4.

Tropman, J. E. (1996). *Making meetings work*. Thousand Oaks, CA: Sage Publications.

Chapter 6
The Effective Meeting: Managing Perspectives

One of the most striking things about meeting masters is their perspective on community meetings. Meeting masters think about their meetings in ways different from accepted convention. Although most group members, community facilitators, and community organizers view community meetings with a sense of hopelessness, meeting masters view them as a mechanism to enact the community's vision.

Seven Principles of Meeting Masters

The philosophy of meeting masters is summarized in the following seven principles. None is complicated or strange. However, the negative culture of community meetings is so deeply entrenched that we complain but cannot stop to make improvements. Each principle has a "caution" section that mentions stumbling blocks that may make these seemingly easy ideas harder to implement.

Purpose Principle

Have a purpose Each meeting or series of meetings that meeting masters are involved with has a purpose stated in writing. The statement of purpose, similar to a vision or mission statement, focuses the group's activities. In addition, the statement brings important differences in perspectives among individuals to the surface early in the process and allows prompt resolution of these.

Caution: Some group members do not want to take the time to clarify purposes. These individuals should be worked with—consulted—before the meeting begins.

Orchestra Principle

Meeting masters regard their meetings as if they are an orchestra or theater performance. There is a score or script (agenda, minutes, and reports) and rehearsal (members working on the material in their minds or holding conversations before the meeting begins, using their "scripts"). If necessary, there are costumes (the ambience created by the meeting dress code and related to roles). (See the "six thinking hats" discussion in chapter 8.) The meeting is seen as the culmination of a preparatory process, not the beginning. One meeting master compared the preparation she did for a meeting to that done for a dinner party at her home. She organizes the tasks so that when the guests arrive everything is ready—the food has been selected, and cooking has begun. She did not tell people as they entered the house, "I wasn't sure what you wanted to eat, so I didn't start anything. I thought I could work that out once you got here." Instead, no effort is spared to create a welcoming, hospitable climate, allowing guests to focus on interaction. The same principle is at work in the orchestra principle. Preparation, organization, and thought can create an outstanding performance.

Think of your meeting as a performance

Caution: Some group members claim they do not have the time to prepare for meetings. They do, but they have other priorities. Remind these members of the four-to-one ratio—four hours are saved for every one hour spent in planning a meeting.

Three-Characters Principle

Focus on announcements, decisions, and brainstorming

Meeting masters believe there are only three things one does at a community meeting—make announcements, make decisions, and brainstorm (discuss and exchange ideas). Meeting masters organize their agendas in that way; meetings are driven by the content or character of the agenda items rather than by the people present. Meetings begin with announcements and then proceed to the items for decision. Work done in advance has identified the items on which action needs to be taken, and appropriate preparatory work has been done. After decisions are made, meeting masters shift to the brainstorming items.

Caution: This principle requires that group members think about the nature of the items they want to discuss, something most never do.

No-More-Reports Principle

Eliminate reports

Many meetings are not meetings at all; they are oral newsletters in which individuals tell what they or their subgroup has been doing. There is no need for this, and meeting masters instead focus on issues.

Meeting masters contact individuals in advance who might want to deliver a report (for example, from a finance or planning committee). The meeting master helps to organize the content along three-character lines. If the content is an announcement, it is given during the announcement section of the agenda. If the content is an item for action or decision, it is put in that section of the agenda. If the item is for discussion and feedback but no decision needs to be made, it is put in the brainstorming section of the agenda. In this way all of the same content is covered but in a more economical and efficient way, with a focus on and identification of exactly what was hoped for when a particular item was introduced. Significant time is saved.

This process differs markedly from the meeting at which a chairperson invites everyone to give a report. In this meeting style, the agenda is driven by those who give reports. These members may have some announcements, some items for decisions, and some items for discussion. Because little thought and organization have been done, even the person who gives the report is sometimes confused about whether an item is up for decision, discussion, or announcement. In this meeting style, every item is already on the agenda and has its place.

Caution: People like to talk. Group members may be attached to their reports and not understand that giving them violates the three-characters principle and can waste time. Meeting masters should work with members on this new style.

No-New-Business Principle

Meeting masters believe that new business is distracting. Typically new business is ill formulated and requires an inordinate amount of time to explore its nature. It can be an invitation for those who are not prepared for the meeting to delay the meeting by focusing on the new business. Meeting masters invite group members to send items for the agenda in advance. This approach puts people in a more thoughtful, more reflective mode when they are suggesting items for discussion and action.

Eliminate new business

Caution: The old style of "show up and spew out" at meetings is deeply ingrained in our culture. To avoid appearing heavy handed, meeting masters can ask group members who want to discuss new topics to wait until the end of the meeting and use what time is left for discussion.

Role Principle

Rewrite participant scripts

When things go wrong in meetings, group members are inclined to blame individuals who they feel have acted inappropriately. Members may feel that if they could only get rid of those meddlesome, troublesome people, the group process would go well. However, the role of the troublesome person is set up in the context of the dynamics of the group, and if that person should leave, somebody else would to step into the role. Problem behaviors can be viewed as roles in the community play. The best way to change roles is to change the script, not the actor. Rescripting the meeting with a carefully prepared agenda and reports will help deal with problems previously thought of as personality differences.

Caution: Finding fault with people is common. Meeting masters have to listen to a lot of off-the-record blaming as a transition to better community meetings.

High-Quality-Decisions Principle

Make good decisions

Meeting masters espouse a deep conviction that a meeting is an information-processing system, the output of which are decisions. They do not view a meeting as a social gathering or a place to chat and meet people, although those things happen. Using the orchestra principle, meeting masters take the view that they get together in meetings to do work, and the work they do is to review information from a variety of sources and make decisions. These decisions must be of high quality. Meetings are not a matter of coming together, quickly making a decision, and adjourning for a cup of coffee; rather, they are deliberate and serious. To emphasize this point, meeting masters sponsor a process of auditing meetings and decisions. For example, groups can look back after a time and examine the decisions they have made. Members can ask, "Here's what we've done during the past six months. Is it any good?" For well-run meetings, the answer will be yes.

This commitment to high quality in the decision-making process creates a sense in the group members that they are doing something important. Looking at the importance of a group fundamentally changes the character of the meetings from a group of people who get together "to take minutes and waste hours" to a group of people who get together to make a difference in their community.

Caution: The idea that a committee ought to actually do something is radical enough; insistence that that "something" be of high quality is an added shocker. However, making high-quality decisions may appeal to committee members, because this concept can be used to drive other committee procedures. People are encouraged to say, "If we want to do something for our community that is worthwhile, here is what we have to do and the ways we have to organize for this to happen."

Conclusion

Managing perspectives is crucial to becoming a meeting master. Meetings run by meeting masters have a sense that expectations are different; before these meetings even begin, they have an aura of success. Productive meetings have a sense of achievement and accomplishment, and this can be reproduced in any group.

Chapter 7
The Effective Meeting: Managing Process

Meeting masters approach community group meetings by addressing four items: planning, preparation, paper, and integrity.

Four items of process

- *Planning.* Meeting masters organize meetings, decide what topics should be on the agenda, and ensure group members have access to the agenda and other information before the meeting.
- *Preparation.* Meeting masters manage preparation. Meeting planning differs from meeting preparation in the same way that meal planning differs from meal preparation. Meal planning focuses on what the menu should be, the components, and people's choices for food. Meal preparation focuses on getting the meal ready just before it is time to eat. Meeting preparation focuses on the order of the agenda and the ordering of items needed for the meeting.
- *Paper.* Meeting masters are sensitive to the volume of paper that group members receive and try to make the amount reasonable, intelligible, and accurate.
- *Integrity.* Meeting masters manage the integrity of the process by honoring time commitments and the agenda.

Managing Planning

Plan

In planning meetings, meeting masters follow three rules: the rule of halves, the rule of sixths, and the rule of three-fourths.

Rule of Halves

Following the rule of halves, community group members can and should give proposed agenda topics and information to the chairperson or community facilitator any time from the end of the last meeting until halfway before the next meeting. Then the chairperson or facilitator, or both, organizes the topics.

Get agenda items ahead of time

For example, a community group that meets every month decides to use the rule of halves. At the end of the January 31 meeting, the chairperson announces that from that time until the middle of February, individuals should consider the items they would like on the agenda for the February meeting and are invited to send those items to the chairperson. At that point in the meeting, someone might suggest that other topics be discussed. The chairperson, with the assistance of the facilitator, keeps a list of those items and others that are proposed after the meeting until the halfway point. At the halfway point, the chairperson and the facilitator meet to sift and sort the topics.

The process of sifting involves determining which items that have been submitted are meeting related. Items are submitted sometimes by people who have personal reasons for suggesting them, and these cannot be handled effectively during the meeting. Those items are set aside and dealt with in an appropriate way, and the individuals who suggested them are informed about the decision. The members get feedback about what happened to their suggestions, and the items do not clutter a full meeting agenda.

Sift agenda items

The process of sorting identifies the character of each item—is it an item for announcement, decision, or brainstorming? Sorting may require contacting the member making the suggestion and obtaining clarification. Sometimes this involves discussing what will happen to the item he or she suggested. The process of crystallization of items adds focus to the agenda.

Sort agenda items

Thought has been given to what will happen to each item submission. The designations of amendments, decisions, or discussion items are not inflexible; however, when proper thought has been given, they allow the chairperson and facilitator to easily set up the agenda.

Rule of Sixths

After agenda items are organized following the rule of halves, they should be tested by the rule of sixths. Approximately one-sixth of the agenda items should be from past discussions; these items still need closure. If past items are more than one-sixth of the agenda, it is likely that the community group is experiencing decision avoidance psychosis, and this problem should be addressed. About four-sixths of the agenda items are current here-and-now type items. About one-sixth of the agenda items are for the future, for example, economic development scenarios or developments in the state that could affect the local community.

Include future items on the agenda

These future agenda items are where group members can have substantial input. Because most groups get items too late in the decision cycle (like coming into a restaurant late in the evening), members' ability to influence the item is often limited (you must eat what the chef has left). However, if items are brought to group members well in advance of their need for closure, the group has decision-making input. Nothing excites members more than the opportunity to see their suggestions, ideas, and perspectives involved in the decision-making process. This creates energy and drive, makes the committee an exciting place to be, and upgrades the quality of participation.

Rule of Three-Fourths

The rule of three-fourths is the mail rule and requires planning and thinking ahead. Meeting masters do not hand out material at meetings but send it ahead of time so that group members can think about the information and come prepared for discussion. The facilitator, having finalized the agenda in consultation with the chairperson, mails the agenda, minutes, and any reports or executive summaries after about three-fourths of the time interval between meetings has passed. For a monthly meeting, three weeks is close enough to the next meeting so that people will read the material, yet not so far ahead of the next meeting that people will set it aside.

Send material in advance

Managing Preparation

With the structure for planning in place and the planning underway, meeting masters spend time in preparation and use the rule of two-thirds and the rule of the agenda bell.

Prepare

Rule of Two-Thirds

The rule of two-thirds divides the meeting into three parts: getting started at the beginning, the heavy work in the middle, and decompression at the end. The decompression begins at approximately the two-thirds point. Hence, during a morning meeting that lasts from 9:00 a.m. until noon, at about 11:00 a.m. the members will begin to lose interest. Meeting masters consider this possible loss of interest when they plan the agenda.

Meeting masters use the three-characters principle to structure the agenda. The first third of the meeting

Go with the flow

begins with the minutes. The minutes are quickly reviewed, any changes noted, and the group moves on. If
there is not a quorum, meeting masters approve the minutes with those who are present and reintroduce them later.
Minutes are followed by announcements—short items
of interest and straightforward statements of unexciting
facts. Exciting facts—things group members will want to
discuss and think about—are saved for the discussion and
brainstorming section. Meeting masters then divide the
decision items into three parts—easy items, moderately
difficult items, and the most difficult items. These items
are arranged in a way as described in Figure 7-1.

Agenda Bell

Agenda bell   Figure 7-1 shows how meeting masters organize items
as suggested by the agenda bell. For example, the minutes are followed by announcements. Then the items
are divided, with the easy items first (items 3a, 3b, and
3c) and more difficult items second (4a, 4b, and 4c),
and each one more difficult than the previous one. The
most difficult item for the meeting is last, and it is placed
between about the 33 percent point and the 66 percent point (or the two-thirds point). After the tough-

Figure 7-1.

The Agenda Bell

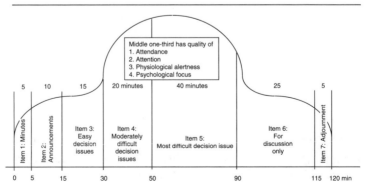

est item is dealt with, the group shifts to discussion and brainstorming items.

Meeting masters use the agenda bell to move issues forward. The meeting can start on time if it begins with minutes; the people who are late have missed little. In addition, people who need to leave early probably will not leave before the two-thirds point. As a result, most group members will be present for all the decision items.

The middle of the meeting, when attendance is greatest and psychological and physiological energy is highest, is when the group is working on its decision-making tasks. Meeting masters use group energy—an often-squandered resource—to help with their tasks. Meeting masters invoke a strategy called "success through small wins." By putting the easy items first, the likelihood of success is higher. The pleasure of success and the desire to leverage success to accomplish more are the underlying dynamics of the ordering of items. This structure is self-reinforcing. Once group members experience the pleasure of accomplishment, they seek it again.

Discussion, which is less intense than decision, can most appropriately take place in the decompression phase when group members are less energized. Discussion has its own re-energizing elements, because the material is exciting topics for the future.

Managing Paper

Meeting masters focus on the paper that individuals receive. In an attempt to inform members, many community groups overinform them with an avalanche of documentation. Often group members set aside these fat packets of information. The problem is that more

Keep paper under control

material means less information. The reverse—less means more—is also true. Meeting masters use the executive-summary technique to lighten the packet and embrace the contradiction.

Executive-Summary Technique

Summaries All reports given to community group members should have an executive summary. When meeting materials are mailed out, the executive summary is sent, not the full report; group members can subsequently request the full report. Thus, a typical information packet consists of the agenda, minutes, and executive summaries (possibly four to six) that agenda topics might require. Members will read such a packet, and although they do not have as much information as a full report, they have key information. Many community groups schedule a half-hour to an hour reading time before the meeting begins to allow members to examine the full documentation of the reports.

The Agenda

Agenda menu Generally phrased items should be avoided in constructing the agenda. More detailed text—like the "dishes" on a restaurant menu—is informative and useful to people. A brief explanation beneath the item will help group members (also like those small explanations below the "dish" on restaurant menus). For example, an item such as "Van purchase agreement" is a good start; a sentence underneath that says, "Finance committee recommends the purchase of six vans at $12,000 each" gives group members more information (see appendix 3 for a sample agenda).

To the right on the agenda one of three key words from the three-characters principle—announcement item, decision item, or discussion item—should be listed. This reminder helps people think about the context in which an item is being offered. The context is different if an item requires a decision rather than just discussion; closure is hoped for in the first instance and openness and freedom in the second.

On the right-hand side of the agenda consider putting a clock. As one meeting master said, "An agenda without a clock is like a menu without prices. It gives you 'that uncertain feeling' that you might have committed yourself to something that you can't really handle." The times on the agenda provide suggested frameworks for the items and show how all the items can be handled (more or less) if the group sticks to them.

Rule of Minutes

Meeting masters give special attention and time to meeting minutes; they use a system called "content minutes" that facilitates the decision-making process, reinforces the process for the group, keeps a record of what happened at the meeting, and encourages completion of tasks agreed on at the meeting. Content minutes (as opposed to process minutes) use a summative reflection paragraph to reflect what happened rather than a narrative of the "he said, she said" variety. The minute taker listens to the discussion and takes notes. However, rather than using specific phrases (except for illustrative purposes), the minute taker prepares a summary of the discussion in which the points are presented logically rather than in the way in which they were spoken during the meeting. Discussion, whether it involves decision issues or the discussion issues themselves, rightfully tends to be unruly and chaotic; an idea strikes someone and he or she shares it, which in turn creates an issue for others, who mention their ideas, and so on. Trying to record everything that everyone said is not a sensible way to record the deeper sense of the meeting. (See appendix 5 for a sample of meeting minutes and chapter 5 for additional discussion of minutes.)

More on minutes

Meeting masters make sure that individuals who have been assigned a task for the next or a subsequent meeting receive a copy of the minutes early, even if the minutes have not been officially approved. In this way the minutes are used as a reminder memo.

Managing Integrity

Respect time commitments   Meeting masters are careful to ensure that time commitments are kept both for the meeting and between meetings. In addition, meeting masters pay attention to agenda integrity and spend time working out the agenda. It would be inappropriate to change the agenda after group members have received it; members will not prepare for the meeting if they know they will not have a chance to discuss the material they have prepared.

Conclusion

Managing the process means paying attention to the details that can derail a meeting. Planning and organizing the agenda are crucial. Sending out the right amount of paper—enough to be helpful but not so much as to be off-putting—is also important. Respecting the work put into the agenda and preparing for it is vital as well. These techniques are not hard to use and pay huge dividends.

Chapter 8
The Effective Meeting: Managing Discussion

Group discussions often produce no results; although there is much talking, no real progress occurs in the decision-making process. Managing discussion to ensure high-quality decisions are reached is an essential part of the successful community process. There are many ways to organize a discussion at meetings. To be effective, discussions must have several elements.

- *Discussions must be based on information.* In most areas of community interest, ample information is available. Some of the information is technical, and consultants and other professionals can help interpret it. Although opinions are important, they should not be a substitute for the facts needed to make high-quality decisions. — **Information**

- *The discussion should be systematic and build toward a decision.* The chairperson, the facilitator, and group members should periodically stop the discussion, check the progress of the group, and organize the next steps. — **Orderly approach**

- *The most productive discussions have a problem-solving nature.* In problem-solving there is a goal to achieve, a decision to make, or a difficult issue to solve. The problem-solving orientation provides a focus for the discussion. Contributions should be encouraged as long as they contribute to progress in problem- — **Problem-solving focus** solving. If needed, a participant can be asked how his or her comment relates to the problem.

Techniques for Discussion Management

Problem–Options–Recommendation

Avoid micro review and rubber stamping

Frequently, a two-step approach is used in the decision-making process. First, a subgroup is assigned a problem and returns with an analysis and a recommendation. The members feel they have done a good job and seek approval. Second, the main group is asked to approve the recommendation. The main group, however, is often getting detailed information about the problem for the first time. As the members examine the recommendation, they are conscious of the need to do a good job and not approve the work of the subgroup without a thorough review. They often want to go over the recommendation in detail. The subgroup may feel as if their work is being questioned and, in a way, it is. This can result in a defensive response from the subgroup that inflames the main group and may convince them that the subgroup is trying to push something past them.

Old two-step approach

These questions and problems result from a lack of understanding about the task at hand and how to go about that task. Therefore, a change in presentation is needed. Instead of the two-step form of problem identification and recommendation, meeting masters recommend a three-step approach.

New three-step approach

This three-step approach (refer to appendix 4 for an example) provides the entire group with information they did not have before: the main alternatives or options that the subgroup worked through and the factors that resulted in the selection of one of them. In this approach, the options are included in the presentation before the recommendation is made. Issues are presented in the following way:

- *The problem*—What is the problem the group is facing?
- *The options*—What are some options available to deal with the problem? (Three to four options are a good number with which to work.)
- *The recommendation*—Which of the options (or combination or sequence of options) does the subgroup recommend and why?

The subgroup outlines these three points in a one-page executive summary. Then, the chairperson or discussion leader invites the main group to examine the recommendation with four questions in mind:

Four key questions

1. Was the *logic* in selecting the recommended option correct?
2. Was the *judgment* correct? (Sometimes logic can be flawless, but judgment is faulty.)
3. Have *errors* remained or crept in that the subgroup did not see? (No subgroup thinks anything of this question if it is part of the regular review.)
4. Can the recommendation be *improved* and, if so, how?

If the group uses these questions, the discussion should proceed smoothly, and each community group and subgroup are focused on the best decision possible.

Avoiding Communication Barriers

Organizing the discussion is a key step in managing discussion. Simply pointing people in the right direction does not always work, however, because barriers interfere with the decision process and make the exchange of information difficult. The following are

Communication barriers

some of the most common barriers in community groups.

An Overdeveloped Sense of Responsibility

"My" issues Some people feel that it is their and only their responsibility to speak for certain issues or certain groups. Effective group discussion allows all members to speak on all issues. Some individuals might have more knowledge than others, but all thoughtful comments are welcome.

Poor Listening

Poor listening Members of a community group often do not listen. Active listening involves attentive behavior with some or all of the following signals:

- eye contact with the speaker
- nods of comprehension as points are explained
- occasional factual and nonhostile questions
- rephrasing and sharing with the speaker to ensure all listeners understand.

Active listening does not occur when people are edgily waiting to get into the conversation, when body language clearly shows disgust with the ideas being presented, or when hostile terms are used. Active listening should be promoted by modeling good listening behavior (Bolton, 1986). Phrases such as "Let's listen carefully to this point . . . even if you do not agree with it" encourage active listening.

Jargon

Jargon Professionals sometimes use jargon that prevents information from reaching others outside their field. The chairperson and others should ask for clarification of an unclear statement that uses jargon; however, no one should make fun of or demean users of jargon, because that creates a defensive response. A better technique is for the chairperson or other leader to rephrase the statement and ask whether the interpretation is correct.

Problematic Styles of Participation

Because some group members like to talk and others are quiet, consideration should be given to all personal styles. However, a personal style should not interfere with the progress of the group (see chapter 2, "Work Styles" and "Learning Styles"). The different styles themselves are not problematic; they become problems when members lack sensitivity concerning the style they have. When vocal individuals talk too much and quiet individuals withdraw, problems occur. Tempering personal style is the solution. For example, tempering the style of the overenthusiastic participator and enhancing the style of the excessively quiet participator is useful and models good behavior.

Participation differences

Avoiding Group Conflict

Structuring the meetings and reports in the ways suggested in this book will reduce group conflict. There will still be conflicts, however, as passions and interests become involved in issues before the community group. Conflict is not always bad, though. Conflicts are like fires in the woods; smaller, more controlled fires are good because they burn off brush and allow new plants—or ideas—to grow. Large, raging fires are not good because the forest—or group—may burn completely.

Conflict

Serious Conflict

The following tips can be used to manage conflict.

Managing conflict

- *Recognize the benefits of limited conflicts.* The group does not have to call the fire department every time a small blaze erupts.
- *Get issues of conflict in the open early, because these issues do not go away.* Failing to address issues of conflict

can lead to partisan solutions, making community solutions harder to achieve. Bringing conflicts into the open early lowers tempers and increases the chance of obtaining a solution that gives everyone something of what they want.

- *Give the opposing parties of the group a chance to resolve issues.* Getting issues in the open early allows subgroups of the opposing parties to reach a joint solution.
- *Use the facilitator and consultants.* Sometimes the facilitator and consultants can meet with the different interests and come up with a win–win idea. The facilitator should be especially helpful when a situation has continued for a while, and community members are locked into their positions.
- *Think win–win.* The chairperson especially has to think and espouse a win–win situation for everyone. It is not always possible for everyone to win, but the culture of the group should be structured so that everyone's interests are part of the solution.
- *Bracket problems.* Although bringing problems into the open early is good, setting a particular aspect of a problem aside—*bracketing*—also should be considered. Setting one part of a problem aside and working on other parts may allow the group, when it returns to the more difficult part of the problem, to find a solution.

Lack of Conflict

Surfacing conflict Sometimes groups appear to have no conflict. However, it is more likely that conflict is being suppressed, and defensive routines are being used. Possibly, a problem such as decision avoidance psychosis, group think, the Abilene paradox, or the boiled-frog phenomenon (see chapter 1) has infected the group. Some conflict is necessary. Without it, important issues may be side-stepped.

Techniques for Discussion

The discussion is one of the most difficult parts of a group to manage, and addressing complex issues may seem impossible. The following techniques can help improve the quality of discussions.

A Useful Template

It is helpful to have a template to organize discussion. **Template**
Several are available, but the following, adapted from the training videotape "Meetings, Bloody Meetings" (Cleese & Jay, 1993), is among the best.

- State and discuss the problem or issue at hand.
- Present various kinds of evidence.
- Discuss the evidence, determine what it proves, and see what people think about it.
- Make the decision and achieve closure.
- Implement and follow up.
- Refine the decision.

Adjust the decision based on implementing experience, that is, revisit it at a future meeting if necessary.

Plan–Do–Check–Act Cycle

In total quality management, the plan–do–check–act **Decision**
cycle can be applied to the decision process. As issues **cycle**
approach, a plan is developed. Then decisions are made, and action ensues. The results of those decisions and actions are observed or checked. On the basis of this information, further action is taken if needed, and the cycle of improvement goes on.

Six Thinking Hats

Sometimes it is hard to get different kinds of thinking **"Color"**
to a problem. Typically, someone plays the devil's ad- **of thinking**
vocate to elicit opinions and encourage people to think.

De Bono (1985) found a way to approach the problem. He invited people in groups to think of themselves as wearing hats of six different colors, each color being associated with a different kind of thinking.

- The *white* hat is neutral and concerned with objective facts and figures.
- The *red* hat suggests anger (seeing red), rage, and emotions.
- The *black* hat is gloomy and negative.
- The *yellow* hat is sunny, positive, optimistic, and hopeful.
- The *green* hat suggests creativity and new ideas.
- The *blue* hat suggests control and the organization of the thinking process.

Using this device, the chairperson does not have to say "You are being too critical. Let's be more positive." An individual may resent that statement and begin a fight. Instead, the chairperson can say, "I have had a good bit of black hat (negative) thinking; perhaps I could have some from the green hat (creativity and new ideas)."

In practice, hats are always referred to by their color and never by their function. The chairperson can ask someone to "take off the black hat for a moment" more easily than he or she can ask that person to "stop being so negative." (For fun, groups can make a set of colored hats available.)

In-Principle Technique

In-principle   The in-principle technique is useful when groups are seesawing between general ideas and details. It helps if the chairperson says at this time, "Let's agree in principle that this is the way we want to do this. We can work out the details by the next meeting." Avoid becoming entangled in details, such as group editing.

Round-Robin Technique

The round-robin technique gets everyone's views in the open before discussion begins by going around the group meeting and giving everyone who wants to a chance to speak. The chairperson can say, "To start this discussion, let's go one by one and share our preliminary views. We'll not discuss them now, just hear them as a way to get started." The chairperson should invite the less powerful members to begin the round robin, thus preventing members with power from dominating the group with their views.

Round robin

Sticky-Dot Voting Technique

The sticky-dot voting technique is a visual demonstration of group preferences and shows how extensive and deep those preferences are. For example, a community group has 26 goals, but they want to have only five main goals for their vision statement. Each of the 26 alternatives is typed on separate sheets of paper, and the sheets are placed around the room. Group members are given five blue sticky dots and one gold dot. The members place their blue dots on the alternatives they feel are important. They can put all five dots on one alternative, four on one and one on another alternative, one dot on five separate alternatives, or any other combination. This accounts for the depth of preference. Then, members put their gold dot on the alternative about which they feel most strongly. The dots are tallied, but it is usually clear which alternative has the most emphasis (the most blue dots) and which is considered the most serious (the most gold dots).

Sticky dots

Straw-Vote Technique

The straw-vote technique is a way to develop a preference ordering for the work of the community facilitator. For example, three or four issues come up in a

Straw vote

meeting that need attention from the community facilitator; however, it is impossible to work on all of them before the next meeting. The chairperson can ask for a "straw vote" from the group about which issues the members think are most important. This vote provides guidance for the facilitator as to where his or her effort should be put.

Conclusion

Managing discussion is an important part of leadership in community process. Using the techniques in this chapter can lead to good discussion. Without good discussion, good decisions are rarely possible.

References

Bolton, R. (1986). *People skills*. New York: Simon & Schuster.

Cleese, J., & Jay, A. (1993). *Meetings, bloody meetings* (videotape directed by Peter Robinson). Chicago: Video Arts.

De Bono, E. (1985). *Six thinking hats*. New York: Little, Brown.

Chapter 9
The Effective Meeting: Managing Decisions

G ood discussions lead to good decisions. Some groups, however, still manage to avoid decisions even when they are close to the decision point. The community leader needs help in assisting groups through the transition of decision.

Closure

Although a community group needs to make decisions, decision making is often avoided (see chapter 1 for a discussion of decision avoidance psychosis). Decision avoidance psychosis saps the group of its sense of accomplishment. Over time, sometimes even a short time, group members conclude that nothing will happen and speak of the group's inability to make decisions with scorn and disdain, even though some individuals might have lobbied hard for decisions to be made. This attitude reflects some group members' approach—avoidance of decision making.

A fundamental responsibility of members and chairpersons is to help the group reach decisions. They should assist the group in discussing and achieving closure and move on to make other decisions. Little that has been discussed in this book will be of assistance unless decisions can be achieved.

Are there decisions?

Decision making involves approach and avoidance

The are many reasons why people avoid making decisions. One reason has to do with not wanting to lose. If somebody gets what they want, somebody else loses. In close communities, people see each other frequently; winners and losers may have to face each other. Losers may be embarrassed; winners may feel guilty. It is one thing to face someone once at a meeting; it is another to see him or her every day. Sometimes it may seem best to step back from a decision and do nothing.

Unfortunately, the nondecision decision *is* something. As a popular poster says, "Not to decide is to decide." In other words, inaction or delay is another form of decision. Sometimes it is the right one. However, it is always better to decide affirmatively to delay than to drift into the decision.

In addition, decisions often are avoided because people perceive them as permanent; the fear that decisions cannot be modified often causes decision avoidance psychosis. Group members often wonder as a decision is approached what the consequences will be if the decision is disastrous. The chairperson must stress and members must understand that decisions are rarely that fateful (see the plan–do–check–act cycle in chapter 8). Although decisions may not be reversed, they can be adjusted, smoothed, and pointed in ways that incorporate new information and perspectives. Decisions often undergo review and improvement. However, this approach can be pushed too far. Group members do not want to review decisions constantly.

Decision Rules

How does resolution occur? Meeting masters learn the slow process of how groups come to decisions, and they know things that others do not. For example, individuals in a group propose an action and are criticized and faulted; it is clear that the proposed action is *not* what the group wants to do. However, meeting masters can listen to a discussion, review the progress, and suggest a course of action. Frequently, group members respond by saying the meeting master's suggestion is the right course of action. What has happened?

This ability of meeting masters to hone in on the key issue or problem is an important skill, because the cacophony of group participation, the disparity of views, and strongly held and opposing positions may not seem to allow for a resolution. How does a resolution that satisfies most of the people in the room happen? The answer involves knowledge about decision rules and the process of decision crystallization (see later in this chapter).

Decision rules—norms from society—are legitimizing rules, and they are accepted as authoritative. In most groups, there are five decision rules—extensive decision rule, intensive decision rule, involvement rule, expert rule, and power rule—that cause conflict. The operation of any rule alone would yield a different set of results than the simultaneous operation of all five. Meeting masters know the decision rules and orchestrate solutions that blend several of the rules simultaneously.

Decision rules make decisions legitimate

Extensive Decision Rule

The extensive decision rule is the most popular or at least most public rule. It refers to one person, one vote, and it tests the breadth of preference. Each individual has the same say, and that some individuals feel strongly about an issue and others do not is irrelevant in the application of the extensive decision rule.

Extensive rule

This rule has been used by everyone. Most groups, however, recognize that there are other rules on which a decision could be based. The extensive decision rule is inadequate unless the group feels that other decision rules and the results that the application of those rules would generate have been addressed.

Intensive Decision Rule

Intensive rule   Some people feel more strongly about some things than others. This depth of preference is never addressed by the extensive decision rule. Groups seek to find out who feels strongly about which issues and, if possible, make some accommodation. Depth of preference is important. Recall the discussion of the sticky-dot voting technique in chapter 8; if a member feels strongly about an alternative, he or she puts all sticky dots on that alternative. In the intensive decision rule, group members try to discover who has strong feelings, so that they can take their strength of preference into account when making a decision.

Involvement Rule

Involvement rule   Most decisions have implementation actions, and sometimes people in the decision-making process are involved in the implementation or have preferences about how the implementation should be carried out. Those who are involved in the implementation usually have more say in the decision than those who are not. In most households, a simple example of this rule is the statement, "The one who has to make dinner gets to pick dinner."

Expert Rule

Expert rule   In many areas (for example, medical care) some issues are known best by experts, and making a decision is not as simple as voting, because the members of the group may not have enough technical expertise. Furthermore, it may not always be clear whether an issue has been addressed by an expert or how convinced that expert might be on the issue. Groups should be aware of what experts are saying with regard to an issue, even if some individuals might not agree with the experts.

Power Rule

In business, the power rule is expressed in the question, "What does the boss think?" In community groups, power is often expressed through social prestige or high occupational position. As a result, powerful individuals in the community have influence, and people want to know what they think.

Power rule

Definition of Consensus

When most groups talk about consensus, they have only a vague idea of what is *really* meant by it. Using the decision rules, we can arrive at a definition. When a proposed decision meets and can be shown to meet these fine rules, consensus has been achieved. The difficulty is that decisions often have to be made on the spot, so knowledge of the decision rules is not always enough. How the rules are used becomes a key skill.

Consensus requires all five rules

Decision Crystallization

Meeting masters help groups make decisions through a process called "decision crystallization." Decision crystallization involves acting on behalf of the group and not on behalf of one's own interests; it involves taking risks, being opposed, stepping back, and engaging in a give-and-take process of constructing a decision. It begins after a period of discussion and goes through rounds of discussion, summative reflection, action hypothesis, vocalization and action legitimization, and discussion refocus.

How are we constructing a decision?

Rounds of Discussion

Rounds of discussion

Meeting masters invite discussion on a topic to begin by asking questions, but not contributing much of their own views. They might express an occasional preference, but they do more listening than talking early in the decision process.

Meeting masters pay attention to rounds of discussion, which occur when each person has made one comment (it could be at the end of a round-robin episode, for example) or when everyone who wants to make a contribution during that round has done so. There is usually a pause at this time, and it is vital that the chairperson or other leader begins the process of crystallization at the end of the first round of discussion, before individuals go into a second, repetitive round. A second round of discussion is not helpful unless some degree of closure has been achieved after the first round.

Summative Reflection

Summative reflection

At the end of the round of discussion, meeting masters begin a *summative reflection*—a summary of where the group stands on a topic during the decision-making process. This reflection allows the group to hear what it has been saying. Many individuals may not remember what everyone else has said during the discussion, which can be a problem if no one is taking time to organize and present in a structured way the ideas that have been discussed. Therefore, summative reflection is an organized approach to the discussion, not just a repeat of what individuals have said. As the chairperson or community facilitator listens, he or she should be organizing the discussion, on paper or in his or her head, and feeding it back to the group.

Action Hypothesis

Action hypothesis

When summative reflection has been completed, the action hypothesis phase begins. A meeting master would say, "The following seems to be a reasonable course of action"; this is how the Abilene paradox (see chapter 1) is avoided. Someone has taken it on himself or herself to voice a suggested action. The hope is that the alternative will be presented and legitimized in such a way as to make it palatable to the group members and thus stimulate agreement.

Vocalization and Action Legitimization

For a group decision to be made, action must be vocalized and legitimized. Vocalization involves the interaction between the person who speaks, working on behalf of the group's interests, and the group members, with their different interests, depth of involvement, expertise, and power.

Vocalization

The immediate next step after vocalization is action legitimization, during which decision rules are put to work. A chairperson may say, "Where should we go for lunch today? The restaurant across the street would be a good place (the action hypothesis), because (the legitimization) most people seem to find that acceptable (extensive decision rule addressed). It has a salad bar for those who do not want to eat meat (intensive decision rule), and John doesn't care where he goes for lunch (involvement rule). They have a new low-fat burger (expert rule), and the boss doesn't care where we spend our lunch money (power rule)." At that point group members give assent with phrases such as, "Sounds like a great idea" and "Fine with me."

Action legitimization

Discussion Refocus

At the decision point, the leader refocuses the group on the next issue, the next step of its business. This process is subtle, but on reflection, individuals who use these techniques will see new methods for group decision making. The risk is that individuals will receive criticism for suggesting an action hypothesis (going on

Discussion refocus

to the next issue). Risks taken on behalf of advancement of the group (as long as it is not a cover for an
advancement of individual interests) and recognized
by the group are rewarded with increased group influence. The process goes on until the entire decision is
constructed.

When a Second Round Is Needed

**What if people
do not agree?**
Suppose the discussion does not go as smoothly as suggested; after the initial advancement of an action hypothesis, the reaction of the group is negative. It was
still useful to advance the action hypothesis, because
during discussion the group learned that the action was
not what they wanted to do. In that case, the facilitator
or chairperson should suggest a second round of discussion but ask people to express preferences different
from those they have already expressed; people should
be invited to stretch their preferences and think of new
ideas, approaches, and opportunities. If this request is
not made, the second round of discussion will be a repeat of the first; everyone will restate what they have
already shared.

After the second round of discussion, the process of
summative reflection, action hypothesis, and vocalization
and action legitimization is repeated. This time, however, the process is more complicated. The chairperson
or facilitator should keep the array of ideas from rounds
one and two together and synthesize opinions from the
two rounds. For particularly difficult issues that require
three, four, or five rounds of discussion, decisions are a
possible but daunting task. Using this process, however,
discussion progresses—builds—toward a decision.

Decision Sculpting

**Decision
sculpting**
When all the smaller parts of the decision have been
made, the group steps back and engages in the final

step in the process. Decision sculpting involves looking at the decision that has been constructed and assessing whether anything has been left out, problems
have been created, or adjustments and alterations are
needed. Once the group members are satisfied that the
decision looks balanced and appeals to a variety of interests, they can move ahead.

Conclusion

The process of managing groups toward decisions is
complicated. Exercising community leadership and
managing toward decisions are complex. Fortunately,
there are techniques and skills that help accomplish
this process. No one is born with these skills; however,
individuals who develop them can help the group make
decisions that work.

Chapter 10
Managing Evaluation

Community management and leadership in the 21st century will be results driven. Businesses, government organizations, and nonprofit organizations are conscious of the need to accomplish tasks. This same drive to achieve results occurs in the volunteer sector and at the board level. Individuals are eager to give their time for community purposes but are unwilling to waste it. If the community leadership program cannot show that it can achieve goals and make progress such that the individuals in the process can experience and enjoy the achievements, there will be a high rate of participant dropout. For this reason, evaluation is a crucial component of community planning activities.

Purposes of Evaluation

Watching "game" films
Evaluation serves two purposes. First, evaluations are a method to review work and determine ways to improve the process. Second, evaluations motivate individuals to do their best work. Group members who know that their performance will be evaluated approach the task with more responsibility, attention, and prudence. Also, people facing an evaluation ask, "Evaluation of what?" The "of what" is the driver for setting goals and objectives.

Sending a message
In addition, an evaluation scheme sends a message to the community: a group that evaluates its work must

be serious about it. An evaluation process can even aid in recruitment of new group members because it sends the message of seriousness.

The presence of an evaluation system is excellent because of its precipitating and predisposing elements that help in both the short and long term. This means that the knowledge that an evaluation system is in place (predisposing factor) and the actual completion of an evaluation process (precipitating factor) work to improve performance in much the same way as having to report their weight at a medical appointment helps people control their eating habits. Care must be taken to ensure the evaluation is not so elaborate that it is unusable or puts people off; an evaluation process should be designed to help.

Predisposing and precipitating factors

Types of Assessment

Three kinds of assessment are worth considering in evaluation. One is a review of each meeting, which helps the individuals who manage the meeting have a sense of what is happening and what needs to be improved. The second is the decision audit, which looks at the range of decisions. The third is the decision autopsy, which examines good and poor decisions in depth.

Meeting Assessment

People should be asked how they feel about the meeting when it is over. One good system for doing this is the KSS (keep, stop, and start) approach.

The KSS approach

Group members should prepare lists with the following information and give the lists to the community facilitator or chairperson. *Keep*: What about this meeting should we keep doing? *Stop*: What about this meeting should we discontinue? *Start*: Are there things in this meeting you did not see that we should start? The facilitator and chairperson should use the suggestions to adjust the content or process of the meeting.

Decision Audit

Decision audit Because decisions are the product of the group meetings, they should be reviewed periodically. The decision audit (and the decision autopsy, discussed later) can be linked to a time schedule or done on an annual basis. The frequency of the audit depends on the turbulence of the group's environment. In a fast-paced environment, the audit cycle should be about every six months or more often. By the time the group discovers that it has been making the wrong decisions in a volatile environment, it is too late to change them. In a tranquil environment, every 18 or 24 months may be acceptable. If a group is seeking to change meeting technology within a slow-moving system, then quick audit cycles are important to reinforce the efforts of the members even though the environment is not turbulent.

Samples from meeting minutes The decision audit requires a good minute-taking system. For the group to review some decisions (perhaps about 20 percent of them), these decisions should be easily accessible. If the minutes have been kept as suggested in this book, decisions will be shaded or boxed and easy to extract. Decisions in the minutes also can be marked with a word-processing file mark or can be indicated with an ampersand or other typographical device that allows all decisions to be pulled from the files automatically. A 20 percent sample then can be easily identified for audit. (Start randomly and then pick the fifth decision thereafter.)

If decisions are difficult to extract from the minutes, the audit may be over as soon as it starts. If the decisions are opaque or unclear or if the keeper of the minutes cannot find the minutes, the group members probably are not sure what happened either.

Once decisions are identified, they should be put on a list, and one to three individuals should grade them, A through F. Criteria or grading are simple:

Grades A–F

- An A is an all-win decision in which all stakeholders are ahead (although they do not have to all be equally ahead). When people say after a meeting, "That was a good decision," they are referring to a decision in which everybody came out ahead. If this were a stock portfolio, all of our stocks would have gone up in value, although not equally.
- A B decision is a plus–minus decision with some stakeholders losing but a larger number of stakeholders gaining. The judgment is that on balance the group is ahead with the decision. For example, it could be a merger in which two executives are now reduced to one. The combined efficiencies and effectiveness of the new operation, however, make that sacrifice of personnel worthwhile. In our stock portfolio, some stocks would have lost money while others gained, but the average gain would be on the plus side of the ledger.
- A C decision is the null decision. Gains and losses have occurred, but the net result is zero. Some people have gained, and some have lost; the system, however, is no farther ahead than it was at the beginning.
- A D decision is the opposite of the B decision. There are some gains and some losses, but there may have been heavy losses in one area (Deming, 1982, called this "incalculable losses"). These losses are not overcome by the positive gains. In our stock portfolio, the overall effect would be entered on the negative side of the ledger.
- The F decision is sometimes called the "nuclear-war decision" or the "all-lose decision." Every stakeholder

is behind where they were before the decisions were made. In our stock portfolio, every stock has lost value.

The reviewers then sum up the grades and present a grade distribution for brief discussion. Although this system is useful, there are other ways to rate decisions. It is the process of decision analysis that is important and not necessarily the system used to make the analysis.

The facilitation of the decision review meeting should be paid considerable attention. The decision audit is not a witch hunt; every effort should be made not to seek guilty parties. If the decision making has not gone well, then efforts can be made to determine— perhaps through the decision autopsy—what the problems are and how they can be corrected. The topics should be introduced for discussion by indicating that the decisions were something common to the entire group; if mistakes were made, everyone made them, and if benefits are attained, everyone shares the glory. Emphasis on team effort and team spirit is essential to make the decision audit work.

Decision Autopsy

Decision autopsy The decision autopsy is a more detailed disassembly of selected decisions—an A decision and an F decision. An in-depth analysis is conducted of what went right (and how to continue successes) and what went wrong (and how to prevent future failures).

It is important to examine an A decision and an F decision for two sets of reasons—psychological reasons and theoretical reasons.

Among the psychological reasons, the A decision and the F decision create the good news–bad news scenario that is beneficial in examining problems. As people know from conducting performance appraisals, it is important to say to individuals, "Here are some things that are going right and that we should continue. In addition, here are some things that are not going well, and we need to look at them in detail and figure out together how we can improve them." Most people feel defensive when things that they are associated with go wrong; there are usually attempts to say, "It's not our fault" and to avoid coming to grips with their own part in the problem. That resistance is lessened if problem areas can be balanced with items that are going well.

Among the theoretical reasons are that things going right and things going wrong appear (but wrongly so) to be at opposite ends of a continuum. Most people think that doing things well is the opposite of doing things poorly. Hence, they make this connection: "If we are doing things well we are, by definition, *not* doing things poorly" (Figure 10-1).

However, a slightly more complicated model is more accurate (Figure 10-2), because most groups perform "success behaviors" *and* "failure behaviors" all the time. Thus, both may be present. For example, assume a group of people are engaged in a range of behaviors; some are successes and some failures. These people perform many of each behavior or some of one behavior but more of another. The key point is that the behaviors are not the same behaviors. Most people do many things throughout the day, personally and in meetings. Some are good, some are bad. In this scenario, a good day is not the opposite of a bad day; it is the average of good and bad behaviors. In the model in Figure 10-2, the upper right quadrant shows where

Figure 10-1.

The Old Paradigm of Success and Failure

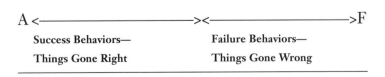

A <————————————————>< ————————————————>F

Success Behaviors—   Failure Behaviors—

Things Gone Right   Things Gone Wrong

Figure 10-2.

The New Paradigm of Success and Failure

```
                    Lots of Success Behaviors
                          9 |
                            |
                          8 |
   High-Quality Enterprises |            Shooting Stars
                          7 |
                            |
                          6 |
```

Few Failure Behaviors   Many Failure Behaviors
    1   2   3   4   5   6   7   8   9

```
                          4 |
                            |
                          3 |
        Lingerers           |               Corpses
                          2 |
                            |
                          1 |
                    Few Success Behaviors
```

individuals, meetings, and even entire firms who are doing many things well and many things poorly are **Shooting stars** placed. They are the shooting stars—they appear to be good at one point but suddenly disappear. Failure caught up with them. Individuals, meetings, and firms that are doing little wrong and most things right are **High-quality enterprises** placed in the upper left quadrant. These are high-quality enterprises. They are doing lots right and little **Lingerers** wrong. In the lower left quadrant are the lingerers— individuals, meetings, and firms that are doing little right but also doing little wrong. They are waiting around for the environment to advance them or finish **Corpses** them off. In the lower right quadrant are the corpses—

those individuals, committees, and firms that have died, although they may not be aware of it.

Groups should be thought of as engaging in bundles of behaviors, the sum of which puts them in one quadrant of Figure 10-2. It is not simply that each behavior is either good or bad. Groups may engage in good behavior and then engage in bad behavior. Together the two behaviors may cancel each other, or the group may perform more good behaviors than bad behaviors. The point is that the F decision involves different behaviors from the A decision. Finding out what the group is doing well and continuing and even improving those behaviors, although important, does not address the other difficulties that groups face—the things they are not doing well. Those poor behaviors are separate and different and must be addressed in their own terms.

Conclusion

These evaluation measures are not in depth; they are designed to give group members the belief that what they are doing is important, has consequences, and will be assessed. These measures give everyone the opportunity to shape the ongoing process and do so in the light of the preferences of the entire group.

Reference

Deming, W. E. (1982). *Out of crisis*. Cambridge, MA: MIT Press.

Part 3
The Rewards of Community Leadership

Communities need leadership now more than ever. Citizens are, if anything, starved for leadership, which is perhaps why fringe groups seem to be so attractive to some. Others retreat—"cocooning" into their houses where they interact only with themselves and a few family members. They work at home, shop from home, watch videos at home, and have food delivered. Both these results, and others, occur in part because community connection cannot be accomplished smoothly and easily. In the absence of community connection, we are drawn into groups that *look like* communities but are actually cults. Or we give up on community completely.

Cohesive, caring communities are vital to an outstanding quality of life. But like anything else, the value of community has to be worth the investment. This is where leadership comes in. Community leadership is the force that creates functioning communities. Functioning communities, in turn, can be connecting and caring and can be where members can place their allegiance. But communities have to be run well; those characterized by ineffective process; rancorous, endless meetings; lack of useful results; and rampant partisanship will soon lose the commitment of their members, who withdraw or drift.

The techniques in this book help people know what to do when they are involved in community leadership. It is a sort of cookbook, with recipes and procedures for making communities better. It is based on the premise that "excellence is never an accident." Well-functioning communities are well functioning because people work at making them so. And as communities function better, tensions are reduced, connection is established, and caring is expressed.

Searching for Information about the Community and Leadership Issues: Using the Library and the Internet

---

By Jessica Schenk, MILS

A number of strategies can be used to seek information. Books, articles, videotapes, and Web sites are useful resources. The trick is knowing where to look for what information. Libraries and the Internet are rich sources of information; however, they also have unique systems that can make it difficult to locate information on a certain topic. Community workers should know how these systems work and how to use them effectively.

Searching in the Library

When beginning research on any topic, the best place to start is the local public or university library. Both have books and indexes that will be useful for

Begin in the library

locating information. A number of computer databases can be useful to search for information; however, each library may have a different system for
conducting searches. Although computer search capabilities vary from library to library, with the larg-
est libraries having the best search capabilities, computers usually can locate books, magazine or journal
articles, and newspaper articles. There may be a different search interface for each computer, although
the interface usually is not difficult to master with
help from the reference librarian. Librarians know
their collections well and can quickly steer researchers toward the information they need.

Libraries are tax-supported institutions, so smaller
communities tend to have smaller libraries. It may be
necessary to visit a large city or university library to
access a larger and more comprehensive collection.
However, this does not mean that small libraries have
nothing to offer. A smaller library may be the best resource depending on the information needed. To take
best advantage of libraries, community workers should
learn what their holdings are and what computer databases they can access.

Books

Card and online catalogs

Books are a great source for general information, and
many have been written on topics of interest to community workers, including how to set up a nonprofit
organization and how to be a good manager. Most people
use the familiar card catalog to find books. People can
open the drawers; flip through the cards; locate a title,
author, or subject; find the call number; and then find
the book on the shelf. Although some libraries still use
traditional card catalogs, most now have computerized
(or online) catalogs to index their books. Computerized
catalogs can still be used to look up books by title, author, or subject. The computerized index provides the

call number and usually indicates if the book is checked out. Online catalogs also allow advanced searches, such as keyword searches, which are useful if the correct subject heading for a topic is not known. A keyword search also can be used to find a book if some of the title words but not the exact order of words is known.

Some people find that online catalogs are difficult to use and take time to learn. However, online catalogs provide more overall flexibility than card catalogs. Online catalogs allow libraries to know what books are on the shelf or are missing or damaged. If the system seems difficult to use, ask the reference librarian for help.

Libraries that do not own a specific title or do not have many holdings on a particular topic often can borrow books from other libraries through the interlibrary loan system.

Magazine and Newspaper Articles

Locating articles on a specific subject from sources other than books can be challenging. Most public libraries have general magazine indexes that organize articles by subject. The *Readers' Guide to Periodical Literature* (1997) is familiar, and it has been the standard magazine index used in libraries for many years. However, many libraries are now purchasing computerized magazine indexes. You may need to ask a librarian how to find magazine articles. In some cases, the index may be integrated with the online book catalog, and in others it may be on a separate computer system.

Magazine indexes

Computerized magazine indexes allow more flexibility in searching. Searches can be run by author, subject, title, or key word. Keyword and subject searches are probably the most popular search strategies for finding magazines, because they tend to yield the greatest results. Another advantage of computerized indexes is that they often allow users to print the full text of the article. Magazine indexes are best to search for current information such as what Congress is doing about environmental problems or how the Supreme Court decided its latest case on sexual harassment.

Newspaper indexes   Newspaper indexes are similar to magazine indexes. Print indexes for individual newspapers have existed for years, and now many newspaper indexes are available on computer. Indexes often cover a range from *The New York Times* to the local newspaper. Computerized indexes allow for flexible search strategies, and the full text of articles often can be printed.

Newspapers are a good source for local information. For example, when looking for ideas for local community fundraising events that were successful previously, newspapers can be the best place to start.

Specialized Resources

Numerous specialized resources are available that may be useful in research.

Government documents

Government documents   Many libraries are federal depositories and receive all or some of the documents published by the federal government. These documents can give the latest information on, for example, Environmental Protection Agency policy. Consult with the local reference librarian for help finding these types of documents.

Legal information

Legal information   Most public libraries have small collections of legal information; the size of the collection depends on the size of the library. However, many law libraries (for example, county law libraries or those affiliated with a law school) exist.

Subject-specific databases

Specialized databases   To search databases such as Social Work Abstracts or Sociological Abstracts, it may be necessary to visit a university or college library. In general, public libraries do not carry as many scholarly resources as university libraries, because they serve different clients. When doing research that requires access to specialized databases, ask a librarian to recommend the best place to go.

General Search Strategies

Library research does not have to be a chore. There are several ways to make the task more interesting.

Search strategies

- *Get to know the librarians and library staff members.* Librarians and library staff know their collections best and can help researchers get started on a search. Librarians also can refer to other nearby libraries that have the information the researcher needs.
- *Become familiar with the libraries in the area.* What does the public library do best? Is there a college or university or law library nearby? Specialty libraries have special collections that may be helpful.
- *Learn to use the library.* Even though much has changed in libraries during the past 10 years, the Dewey decimal system is still used, along with a catalog for books and indexes for magazines and newspapers. Although it may seem overwhelming at first, learning the basic layout of the library and how materials are indexed and classified does not take long.
- *Ask for help when needed.* Reference librarians are paid to help library users find information, so take advantage of their expertise and experience.

Browsing the Internet

The Internet has millions of sites. Browsing the Internet can be fun but also can be a waste of time. How is it possible to easily find sites relevant to a particular research project? As with using libraries,

Browse the Internet

researchers need fundamental skills to use the Internet effectively. If some time is taken initially to learn, the task of searching the Internet will be easier.

Background

The Internet and the World Wide Web

The Internet is a worldwide network of computers that can communicate with each other. For example, if a person in Michigan wants information located on a computer in England, all he or she has to do is make the request. The computer in Michigan asks the computer in England for the information and, assuming there are no breakdowns in the network on either end, the requested information is sent from England to Michigan. The user may need to know what commands to type into the computer to initiate the request or may simply hit a few clicks of a computer mouse.

The most popular part of the Internet is the World Wide Web, primarily because of its ability to integrate text, graphics, sound, and video. The Internet also has electronic mail and file transfer capability.

To learn more about the Internet, the final step is to get connected. Frequently, public libraries provide access to the Internet and often do not charge members of the local community for use. If this is not an option, many national and local companies, called "Internet service providers," offer access to home and business users. Companies such as America Online and Prodigy are nationwide Internet service providers. There are also numerous local Internet service providers. One place to find a provider is on the Internet at http://www.thelist.com/. Telephone companies also are providing Internet service, so it might be worthwhile to check with them, too. Ask Internet users in the community which service providers they use and whether they are happy with their service.

After getting connected, the question to answer is, "Where can I look for more information about the Internet?" Books are an excellent source of information,

Figure A1-1.
URL Format

and hundreds have been published about the Internet. Check the local library or bookstore. Newspapers, magazines, and trade publications are also good sources of information. Today, many television commercials and print advertisements include a World Wide Web address for the company doing the advertising. Local newspapers often print lists of local Internet service providers, and magazines sometimes publish articles on the "Top 10 Internet sites of the year" by category. With a little work, a researcher can find much useful information.

Next is "surfing the 'Net." To be a successful **Surf the 'Net** Internet researcher, two questions should be answered: (1) What are the best search tools to pinpoint information on a specific topic, and (2) When searching, how is it possible to determine if the information found is good information?

Figure A1-1 explains some Internet addressing conventions. Internet addresses are formatted by uniform resource locators (URLs), so it is possible to determine some information about the site just from the address.

"Type of resource" is the type of Internet resource referred to in the address. In the figure, "http" (hypertext transfer protocol) is the World Wide Web address. Other protocols include "mailto," which refers to an e-mail address, and "ftp" (file transfer protocol), which refers to a file available for transfer.

The computer name usually takes the form of host.institution.domain and indicates where the information is being stored. "Host" and "institution" generally refer to the name of the computer that hosts the information and the institution where the computer is located. "Domain" refers to the type of institution or the country, or both, in which the computer is located. The *.org domain name indicates an organization, *.com indicates a commercial entity or corporation, and *.edu indicates an educational institution (in computer file names, the asterisk [*] is called a "wild card" and can represent any name). Internet addresses that originate outside the United States might have names such as *.ca for Canada or *.mx for Mexico or *.uk for the United Kingdom.

The directory name indicates where on the computer the information is located. The file name is the name of the file that you want to read.

Useful Internet Addresses

Useful addresses The sample Internet sites in Table A1-1 can be accessed by using the "open" command on a browser (such as Netscape or Internet Explorer). A good resource for community-related Web sites is the *Chronicle of Philanthropy's Non Profit Handbook,* which is published every year (1255 23rd Street, Washington, DC 20037; 202-466-1227).

Searching for Information on a Specific Subject

Subject Guides

Subject guides A subject guide is a collection of Internet sites that have been examined and classified in a database (see Table A1-2). Subject guides allow access to a smaller database

Table A1-1.

Sample Online Sites

Site	Internet Address
Alliance for National Renewal	http://www.ncl.org/anr/index.htm
Center for Policy Alternatives	http://www.cfpa.org/
Chronicle of Philanthropy	http://www.philanthropy.com
Decision Analysis Society (from Duke University)	http://www.fuqua.duke.edu/faculty/daweb/
Facilitator Central (from Baylor University)	http://hsb.baylor.edu/fuller/fac/
HandsNet on the Web	http://www.handsnet.org/
Institute for the Study of Civic Values	http://libertynet.org/~edcivic/iscvhome.html
Meeting Guide	http://www.mmaweb.com/meetings/
National Association for Community Leadership	http://www.communityleadership.org/
National Civic League	http://www.ncl.org/ncl/
National Community Building Network	http://ncbn.org/welcome.shtml
Nonprofit FAQ (frequently asked questions)	http://www.nonprofit-info.org/npofaq/
Nonprofit Resources Catalogue	http://www.clark.net/pub/pwalker/home.html

of sites compared with search engines (see following discussion). For that reason, subject guides are often a great place to start a search. The resulting lists from the search will be smaller and more manageable, and it will be easier to evaluate the quality of the material retrieved.

Table A1-2.

Sample Subject Guides

Guide	Internet Address
Galaxy	http://www.einet.net/
Yahoo	http://www.yahoo.com/
Magellan	http://www.mckinley.com/
Lycos A to Z	http://a2z.lycos.com/

Search Engines

Search engines Search engines search huge databases of Internet sites that have been indexed by computers (see Table A1-3). Because these databases are compiled by computers, they can be much larger than those that require human input. These search engines can be particularly useful when looking for information on an unusual or obscure topic. Search engines often allow for more sophisticated search methods than do subject guides, so they may be a better choice when some degree of precision is important (for example, phrase searching).

Librarian-Organized Sites

Librarian-organized sites Librarian-organized sites are designed and maintained by information professionals (see Table A1-4). These sites were created and designed by librarians who

Table A1-3.

Sample Search Engines

Search Engine	Internet Address
Alta Vista	http://www.altavista.digital.com/
Excite	http://www.excite.com/
Hotbot	http://www.hotbot.com/
Infoseek	http://www.infoseek.com/
Lycos	http://www.lycos.com/
Open Text Index	http://index.opentext.net/
Webcrawler	http://webcrawler.com/

Table A1-4.

Sample Librarian-Created Sites

Site	Internet Address
Internet Public Library	http://www.ipl.org/
Michigan Electronic Library (useful to any searcher)	http://mel.lib.mi.us
Argus Clearinghouse	http://www.clearinghouse.net/

wanted to apply their skills for organizing information to the Internet. Librarians know what information will be most useful for their clients. Now, librarians are using their skills to determine what information on the Internet will be most useful to users of the Internet. These databases also may be smaller than the computerized indexes. The main advantage to these sites is that the quality of information is the focus instead of the quantity of information. Although these sites provide a search mechanism for users, it often helps to browse by subject area. For any research project, these sites are a great place to start. The option of searching a larger database is available if additional information is needed.

General Search Strategies

The number of databases available for searching the Internet continues to grow. The lists shown in Tables A1-1 to A1-4 are only small examples of each type of database. Each is different in terms of indexing and searching techniques. It is important to find a database that feels comfortable and intuitive and then learn it well. Some general search strategies can be useful when getting started:

Search strategies

- One way to compare databases is to conduct the same search in each and compare results. Which was the most successful?
- Users should carefully read any instructions provided by the database developer. These instructions will guide the user in formulating the best searches.
- Databases do not automatically index all sites on the Internet. In most cases, the developer of the information is required to submit the site to a database service for it to be indexed. If a company or organization develops a site but does not submit it to any of the database services, it might be impossible to learn of its existence.
- Internet databases are not sophisticated search tools and have a way to go to catch up with their CD-ROM counterparts. Part of the problem is that Internet databases index resources stored on computers all over the world, whereas CD-ROMs are self-contained resources.

The best way to demonstrate the different Internet search tools is to show some sample searches. Table A1-5 shows the results of a basic search run in all of the subject guides and search engines listed in Tables A1-1 to A1-3 (the librarian-organized sites are not included because their search and retrieval functions are set up differently). The table is not a scientific comparison of databases; it is intended to provide an overall impression of the differences of each. The subject guides retrieved far fewer sites than the search engines.

The search terms used were *homeless michigan*. In each case the terms were entered in exactly the same order without quotes or connector words such as "and," "or," or "not." In some cases, the results could have been refined by using advanced search options.

Evaluating Information

Researchers should evaluate any information retrieved from the Internet. Anyone can publish information on the Internet, and it is important to be able to determine what value, if any, information has. The following are key points to consider when evaluating a site:

Evaluating information

- Who is the authority responsible for publishing the information?
- Is the information up-to-date (is it even dated)?
- Are proper citations used for data or information presented? Is credit given where appropriate?
- Is the information presented for factual purposes or to prove a particular point?

If the answers to these questions are not obvious, it might be a good idea to try a new site.

Videotapes and Films

Videotapes and films can be excellent sources of information because they can demonstrate techniques more clearly than the printed word. Both can be found at the local library.

View videotapes and films

Some examples of videos include

- *The Abilene paradox.* (1974). By CRM Productions. Carlsbad, CA: McGraw-Hill Training Systems.
- *Groupthink.* (1991). Written and produced by Kirby Timmons and produced by Melanie Mihal. Carlsbad, CA: CRM Films.
- *Introduction to social movements.* (1995). By Mayer Zald. Ann Arbor: University of Michigan, ICOS.
- *The leader.* (1988). Lake Orion, MI : Encyclopaedia Britannica Educational Corporation.

Table A1-5.

Sample Comparison Searches

Search Tools	Number of Sites	First Site on List
Alta Vista	70,000	Michigan's Homeless Shelters http://www.nmc.edu/~lanninl/mich.htm
Excite	453,604	National Homeless Awareness Week (message posted to a newsgroup) http://csf.colorado.edu:80/lists/homeless/nov96/0078.html
Galaxy	14	American Relocation Center http://www.sover.net:80/~relo/
Hotbot	6,656	Musical Feast[a] http://www.musicalfeast.com/
Infoseek	323,386	Michigan's Homeless Shelters http://elmo.nmc.edu/~lanninl/mich.html
Lycos	12,461	Michigan Comnet http://comnet.org/index.html
Lycos A to Z	165	Michigan Web Servers http://www.w3.org/pub/DataSources/www/Michigan.html
Magellan	44,259	Homeless Help http://www.freenet.org/gdfn/wayne/helping/homeless.htm
Open Text Index	262	Michigan League for Human Services http://pilot.msu.edu/user/mlhs/
Webcrawler	23,491	Directory of State and National Homeless/Housing Organizations http://nch.ari.net/direct.html
Yahoo	2	Michigan Comnet http://comnet.org/index.html

[a]The Musical Feast site was selected because it was promoting a cookbook with recipes from famous musicians. Proceeds from the book are to benefit the homeless population. One of the musicians in the cookbook is Madonna, who is from Michigan.

- *More bloody meetings: The human side of meetings.* (1984). Written by Anthony Jay and directed by Charles Crichton. Chicago: Video Arts.
- *Straight talking: The art of assertiveness.* (1991). Chicago: Video Arts.
- *Think or sink.* (1991). Chicago: Video Arts.
- *Valuing diversity.* (1987). San Francisco: Copeland Griggs Productions.

Reference

Reader's guide to periodical literature. (1997). New York: John Wiley & Sons.

Appendix 2
The Disabled Women's Project: Lessons in Community Leadership

By Carla Parry

This case study examines a community-organizing effort that at first failed. Although the premise of the organization was sound and the intentions of those involved were sincere, a lack of leadership, planning, and knowledge of organizing skills caused the project to disintegrate. The disappointment and frustration of the group could have been avoided if the directors of the project had followed the guidelines in this book. This case study shows the problems of community work and solutions to those problems, which are discussed in this book.

Background

Battered women with disabilities are vulnerable and isolated members of society. About 60 percent of women with disabilities are subjected to abuse at some point, and many women experiencing domestic violence become permanently disabled from battering episodes. Battered women with disabilities are a diverse group and have a range of disabilities of mobility or visual impairments, epilepsy, asthma, osteoporosis, mental illness, and learning. Many women have multiple disabilities or disabilities such as traumatic brain injuries and hearing impairments that were directly caused by battering. However, women with disabilities are underrepresented in battered women's shelters because many shelters are not accessible for people with disabilities or do not provide programs and services that address the complex needs of women with disabilities.

In 1982 a small grassroots nonprofit organization formed to address these issues. The Disabled Women's Project (DWP), founded by a disabled woman in a large western city, supported five battered women's shelters and a variety of services for people with disabilities. DWP began as a crisis hotline for battered women with disabilities and was initially operated by the founder. For 10 years, DWP grew slowly until it reached its current size of three full-time staff, two part-time staff, and 12 volunteers, with an annual budget of $100,000.

DWP initially served as a liaison between battered women's shelters and the disability community. As DWP developed, it provided in-depth case management, emergency financial assistance, crisis counseling, and information and referral services to clients and technical assistance and education to agencies that serve battered women and people with disabilities. Later, DWP began to act as an advocate for battered women with disabilities who were denied access to shelters as a result of attitudinal or physical barriers. Many battered women's shelters were insensitive to the needs of disabled women and were not knowledgeable about resources available to people with disabilities. Relations between the shelters and DWP were sometimes strained, because the shelters had little interest or investment in becoming accessible to women with disabilities. Efforts to educate shelter workers and volunteers about disability awareness were discouraging, because the high turnover rate of executive directors, staff, and volunteers in the shelters made it necessary to provide constant training.

Access Coalition I

To address the issue of shelter inaccessibility in a community forum, in 1993 DWP facilitated the formation of the Access Coalition. DWP's director envisioned the coalition as an informal forum at which community services providers from the battered women's community and the disability community could share resources and develop strategies to better serve battered women with disabilities. The Access Coalition was initially welcomed, but within a year it had crumbled. At first attendance dropped; later the shelter representatives stopped attending the meetings. Soon the coalition had deteriorated to a group of advocates from disability organizations who met irregularly to gripe about shelter inaccessibility. The reasons the coalition failed are clear.

Good intentions and commitment were not enough to make the coalition work. Moreover, DWP did not follow the basic guidelines of community leadership. The lead organization failed to engage the stakeholders in the community, to develop a clear blueprint for the coalition, to diffuse the antipathy between the disability and shelter communities, and to take leadership. As a result, the Access Coalition did not engender trust or commitment in its membership and ultimately became a hostile discussion group rather than an action forum. The primary causes of the coalition's downfall were problems of procedure, problems of process, and problems of people, as well as disregard for the ground rules for committee and group work.

The problems of procedure were a result of a lack of clearly defined mission; the coalition also lacked purpose, process, structure, and leadership. Without a clearly articulated purpose and procedure, it was easy for the coalition to veer off course and ultimately disintegrate.

The Access Coalition also experienced problems of process. The coalition fell victim to decision avoidance psychosis because coalition members were unsure of the purpose of the coalition and because DWP had chosen coalition members randomly, not including all four components of the garbage can model of community choice: problem knowers, problem solvers, resource controllers, and decision makers looking for work. The coalition was composed only of problem knowers and resource controllers. Thus, the coalition became a forum in which problem knowers tried to convince resource controllers of the existence of a problem, and resource controllers questioned how changes might be implemented. Because it lacked problem solvers and decision makers, the coalition frustrated everyone involved.

The greatest detriment to the Access Coalition, however, was its problems of people. The coalition included only representatives from small nonprofit organizations, mostly allies of DWP in the shelter and disability communities. Many of the members of the coalition were inexperienced or were staunch partisans of various causes who were not able to assume the role of statesperson in community discussions. Key stakeholders and power brokers in the community either were not invited or chose not to attend the forum. Little change or problem solving could occur without the representation of those in power. The greatest people problem, however, was the inexperience of DWP in leading a community group. By failing to mediate discussion and to provide leadership and direction to the group, DWP allowed the coalition to become a hostile and unproductive forum.

The Access Coalition met its demise because of failure to adhere to the ground rules for committee and group work. Although time commitments were honored, the coalition did not respect the agenda (because a formalized agenda did not exist), leadership, and people and ideas.

Access Coalition II

Once DWP became aware of the reasons for the failure of the Access Coalition, it attempted to create a second coalition, this time using the techniques of effective leadership. DWP first assumed the roles of researcher and documentor of the problem of shelter inaccessibility to women with disabilities (see chapter 5). In the next two years, DWP completed access surveys of all battered women's shelters in the state and a needs assessment in the local community. The accessibility surveys revealed that less than 25 percent of the shelters in the state were even marginally accessible to battered women with disabilities. The needs assessment showed that high numbers of women with disabilities were being routed to homeless shelters and hospitals instead of battered women's shelters and that many women with hidden disabilities were routinely denied services from shelters. Instead of criticizing the shelters for their inaccessibility, DWP focused on providing support to the shelters

in the form of volunteer and staff disability awareness
training, community education, and the provision of
advocacy to battered women with disabilities in the shelter system. Providing assistance and education served
to build rapport and resurrect relationships that were
damaged in the fallout of the first coalition.

DWP identified locations of power, carefully identi-
fying and assessing individuals, organizations, and institutions that might be useful allies in soliciting support for the Access Coalition and its goals or that might
be enemies or impediments to change. By tracking patterns of resource control and service delivery, DWP was
able to identify stakeholders (see chapter 2). Coalition
members were chosen from a broad range of organizations and auspices. DWP ensured that the second coalition was more diverse than the first, including both
nondisabled people and people with disabilities as members, as well as representatives from small and large agencies. The key stakeholders included shelter directors,
board members, counselors, shelter client and legal advocacy staff, housing and referral programs, disability groups that aid with subsidized and emergency housing, emergency attendant care programs, transportation
services, transitional benefit program officers, program
officers for Supplemental Security Income and disability income, various disability-specific groups (such as
the Epilepsy Foundation), consultants in access and
training with regard to the Americans with Disabilities
Act, and formerly battered women with disabilities.

With research and documentation in place and the
stakeholders engaged, DWP appointed a community
organizer to act as the coordinator–manager of the
coalition (see chapter 5) and revived the Access Coalition in 1995. The purpose of the coalition was out-
lined: to eradicate barriers to shelter accessibility while
strengthening the connections between the shelter and

disability communities. DWP defined its role as a conduit and organizer of resources between disability organizations, consultants, and shelters.

DWP set ground rules for the process, goals, outcomes, leadership, and expectations of involvement and commitment from members. An important consideration in counteracting adversarial and apathetic responses was DWP's approach; DWP realized it needed to work at reducing defensiveness among the shelters and reducing attack responses from disability-rights groups. Careful consideration of the history of interactions between these groups suggested that sensitive facilitation and the creation of an open atmosphere for discussion were crucial to the success of the project. The second coalition invited members from the community to attend monthly meetings that provided education about accessibility, resources for serving battered women with disabilities, opportunities to network with disability service groups, and the opportunity for shelters to share solutions that they had devised to the problems encountered by battered women with disabilities.

Lessons Learned

The lessons learned from the two attempts to form the Access Coalition are lessons in leadership. Good intentions and a good idea were not enough to make the first coalition a success; attention to process, procedure, and people engendered trust in the coalition and allowed it to become an effective community group and a vehicle for change.

Most important to the coalition's success was attention to issues of people. "Disabiliphobia" was present in the first Access Coalition insofar as some nondisabled coalition members were uncomfortable working with people with disabilities and were not knowledgeable about the issues and concerns of the disability community. It may also have been disabiliphobia that made the shelters sensitive to critiques of their accessibility and subsequently raised tensions between the shelter and disability communities. The greatest people problem, however, was the lack of skills and competency of the lead organization in carrying a project like the Access Coalition. By learning leadership skills and appointing a community organizer with solid interpersonal skills to manage the coalition, these problems were mitigated.

Appendix 3
Sample Agenda

To:	Community Group
From:	Pam
Re:	Community Meeting, Monday, 10 a.m. to noon
Date:	"Any Monday"

1. Announcements   10:00–10:10

Penny, Sarah, Matt, Jessica

2. Minutes from last meeting   10:10–10:15

3. Easy Items (Decision)   10:15–10:35

   3a. Main Street decoration—Penny   10:15–10:25
      The same firm is recommended
      to do the work as last year.

   3b. New music programs—Matt   10:25–10:35
      Matt recommends we invite the
      Marine Band from Washington,
      DC, for summer festival.

**4. Moderately Tough Items
(Decision)**   10:35–11:05

   4a. Breast cancer alert—Sarah   10:35–10:50
      Mammography sites will be
      set up around town.

   4b. Community archives—Jessica   10:50–11:05
      Review and approval is needed
      of new information system.
      (Attachment A)

5. Tough Item (Decision)   11:05–11:30

Approve negotiations for child
welfare agency merger.

6. Blue-Sky Items (Discussion Only) 11:30–12:00

> Look at new issues.

6a. Community Health Needs Software—Matt
6b. Health online—Jessica
6c. The health care system—Sarah

Snack follows at noon!

Appendix 4
Sample Options Memo

The Problem: Community Archives

Multiple storage locations for important documents
Key needs-assessment reports for the community are stored in several agencies. A master file system has not yet been set up. There is lack of understanding about what should be stored and conflict over common locations. Thus, access is inhibited.

The Options

1. Let things stay as they are for now.
2. Plan to revisit this problem in six months.
3. Ask Jessica to develop a plan for selection, storage, and access.

The Recommendation—Option 3

Jessica should be asked to develop a plan for selecting key documents and proposing a common storage location. In addition, she should propose ideas to improve access. Any delay means more will be lost and the job will be tougher.

Appendix 5
Sample Minutes

1. Announcements

Penny announced the new slot in the parking lot was now available for community meeting members. Sarah announced a new program at Woman's Health, Inc. Matt announced he would be at a software meeting on Friday. Jessica announced new materials for the library.

2. Minutes from Last Monday's Meeting

The minutes for the last meeting were accepted.

3. Decision Items

3a. Community Decoration
The firm used last year was thought to be satisfactory; there is no price increase for this year.

> **Decision:** We will go with the same firm.

3b. New Music Program
Matt knows several people in the President's own Marine Band in Washington, DC. He feels it is possible to get on their tour schedule.

> **Decision:** Matt will obtain information for next meeting.

4a. Mobile Mammography
Problems have occurred in the community because women live too far from mammography services. Sarah

has arranged for portable mammography units to be available on a preannounced schedule.

> **Decision:** The mobile mammography plan was approved.

4b. Community Archives
There was discussion of the community archives report.

> **Decision:** It was decided to ask Jessica to proceed to develop a plan; she reports back in six months.

5. Child Welfare Agency Merger Negotiations

Given the economic climate, it seemed useful for our community group to urge the two child welfare agencies in town to explore merger possibilities. Both are opposed; neither is interested in even talking to the other. This resistance was taken as an excellent reason to proceed. Others reasons include community complaints about each, the shabby quarters each has, and the real possibility of running one excellent organization.

> **Decision:** It was decided to proceed with the proposal to suggest merger talks begin.

6. Blue Sky Items—New Markets

A lively discussion of new issues (software, health online, and health care settings) was held. Each of these seemed promising. More discussion will be held next month.

Further Reading

Carver, J. (1990). *Boards that make a difference.* San Francisco: Jossey-Bass.

Cleese, J. (1988, May 16). No more mistakes and you're through. *Forbes,* p. 26.

Clifton, R. L., & Dahms, A.I.A.M. (1980). *Grassroots administration: A handbook for staff and directors of small community-based social service agencies.* Prospect Heights, IL: Wavelin Press.

Conrad, W. R., Jr., & Glen, W. E. (1983). *The effective voluntary board of directors.* Athens, OH: Swallow Press.

Duca, D. (1986). *Nonprofit boards.* Phoenix: Oryx Press.

Fisher, R., & Ury, W. (1981). *Getting to yes.* New York: Penguin.

Goodman, P. S., & Associates. (1986). *Designing effective work groups.* New York: Jossey-Bass.

Greenleaf, R. (1973). *Trustees as servants.* Peterborough, NH: Windy Row Press.

Houle, C. (1989). *Governing boards.* San Francisco: Jossey-Bass.

Janis, I. (1972). *Victims of groupthink.* Boston: Houghton-Mifflin.

Janis, I. (1989). *Crucial decisions.* New York: Free Press.

Janis, I., & Mann, L. (1977). *Decision making: A psychological analysis of conflict, choice, and commitment.* New York: Free Press.

Kieffer, G. D. (1988). *The strategy of meetings.* New York: Warner.

Margolis, R. J. (1989, September). In America's small town hospitals. *Smithsonian,* pp. 52–67.

Mosvick, R. K., & Nelson, R. B. (1985). *I've got to start meeting like this.* Glenview, IL: Scott Foresman.

Muller, R. K. (1977). *Metadevelopment: Beyond the bottom line.* Lexington, MA: Lexington Chapters.

Muller, R. K. (1981). *The incompleat board.* Lexington, MA: Lexington Chapters.

Myers, R. J., Ufford, P., & McGill, M. S. (1988). *Onsite analysis: A practical approach to organizational change.* Etobicoke, Ontario: On Site Consulting Associates.

Naisbett, J., & Auberdene, P. (1985). *Reinventing the corporation.* New York: Warner.

Ott, J. S., & Shafritz, J. M. (1986). *The Facts-on-File dictionary of nonprofit organization management.* New York: Facts-on-File Publications.

Parkinson, C. H. (1985). *Parkinson's law.* London: Oxford.

Plous, S. (1993). *The psychology of judgement and decision making.* New York: McGraw-Hill.

Portnoy, R. A. (1986). *Leadership: What every leader should know about people.* Englewood Cliffs, NJ: Prentice Hall.

Schmid, H., Dodd, P., & Tropman, J. (1987). Board decision making in human service organizations. *Human Systems Management, 7,* 155–161.

Solomon, L. D. (1978). Restructuring the corporate board of directors: Fond hope—Faint promise? *Michigan Law Review, 76,* 581–601.

3-M Meeting Management Team. (1994). *Mastering meetings.* New York: McGraw-Hill.

Tichy, H., & Devanna, M. A. (1986). *The transformational leader.* New York: John Wiley & Sons.

Tjosvold, D. (1986). *Working together to get things done.* Lexington, MA: Lexington Chapters.

Toseland, R., & Rivas, R. (1984). *An introduction to group work practice*. New York: Macmillan.

Tropman, J. E. (1982). The decision group: Ways to improve the quality of meetings and decisions. *Human Systems Management, 3,* 107–118.

Tropman, J. E. (1995). Community needs assessment. In R. L. Edwards (Ed.-in-Chief), *Encyclopedia of social work* (19th ed., Vol. 1, pp. 563–569). Washington, DC: NASW Press.

Tropman, J. E. (1995). *Effective decisions in meetings*. Beverly Hills, CA: Sage Publications.

Tropman, J. E. (1996). *Effective meetings: Improving group decision making* (2nd ed.). Beverly Hills, CA: Sage Publications.

Tropman, J. E., Erlich, J., & Rothman, J. (Eds.). (1995). *Tactics and techniques of community intervention* (3rd ed.). Itasca, IL: F. E. Peacock.

Tropman, J. E., Johnson, H. R., & Tropman, E. J. (1991). *Committee management in the human services* (2nd ed.). Chicago: Nelson-Hall.

Tropman, J. E., & Moringstar, G. (1989). *Entrepreneurial systems for the 1990s*. Istport, CT: Quorum Chapters.

Waldo, C. N. (1985). *Boards of directors: Their changing role, structure, and information needs*. Istport, CT: Quorum Chapters.

Waldo, C. N. (1986). *A working guide for directors of not-for-profit organizations*. New York: Quorum Chapters.

Weick, K., & Roberts, K. (1993). Collective mind in organizations: Heedful interrelating on flight decks. *Administrative Science Quarterly, 38,* 357–381.

Zander, A. (1982). *Making groups effective*. San Francisco: Jossey-Bass.

Zelman, W. (1977). Liability for social agency boards. *Social Work, 22,* 270–279.

Index

About the Author and the Contributors

The Author

John E. Tropman, MSW, PhD, is professor, School of Social Work, University of Michigan, where he teaches in the areas of human services management, community organization, and social policy, and in the joint doctoral program in social work and social science. He has written and edited a number of books in the areas of management, community organization, and social policy. Creating and sustaining caring, constructive communities through the appropriate leadership has been one of his lifetime interests.

The Contributors

Jessica Schenk, MILS, is librarian and head, Systems and Technology Division, Novi Public Library, Novi, Michigan. An information specialist, she was instrumental, along with others, in creating the Internet Public Library. In addition to her work at Novi, she designs Web pages.

Carla Parry, MSW, is doctoral student, joint doctoral program in social work and social science, University of Michigan. Her areas of interest include services to disadvantaged people, women's issues, and organizational structure.

Successful Community Leadership:
A Skills Guide for Volunteers and Professionals

Cover design by Naylor Design, Inc.

Interior design by Naylor Design, Inc.

Composed by Melissa Conroy, Wolf Publications, Inc.,
in Ja on and Univers

Printed
Windsor Offset

ORDER THESE HOW-TO BOOKS ON COMMUNITY FROM NASW PRESS

Successful Community Leadership: *A Skills Guide for Volunteers and Professionals,* by John E. Tropman. With this practical how-to manual, you'll learn new techniques and skills to help your community group work cohesively and successfully. Whether you work with communities large or small, you'll find this guide indispensable in helping members define, act on, and achieve their objectives.

ISBN: 0-87101-285-5. Item #2855. Price $25.95

Community Building: *Renewal, Well-Being, and Shared Responsibility,* Patricia L. Ewalt, Edith M. Freeman, and Dennis L. Poole, Editors. In this timely new source book, you'll learn how you can help community members identify their needs in areas that include the physical environment, housing, economic opportunity, safety, education, and health care.

ISBN: 0-87101-292-8. Item #2928. Price $29.95

Organizing: *A Guide for Grassroots Leaders, Revised Edition,* by Si Kahn. *Organizing* is a dynamic guide on how to unite people for change, to help people work together to get things done. It describes how to influence power structures and how to become successful organizers and fundraisers.

ISBN: 0-87101-197-2. Item #1972. Price $32.95

How People Get Power, *Revised Edition,* by Si Kahn. *How People Get Power* can help organizers and community leaders bring unity and success to those they serve. Kahn describes how an effective organizer enables others to improve their lives by convincing naysayers, persuading policymakers, and using self-determination to create change.

ISBN: 0-87101-236-7. Item #2367. Price $20.95

Issues in International Social Work: *Global Challenges for a New Century,* M. C. Hokenstad and James Midgley, Editors. In this timely volume, you'll get a briefing on the critical issues in international social work at the dawn of the 21st century. You'll learn about the place of social work in a global economy, the contribution of social work to social development, the role of social workers in addressing ethnic conflicts, future directions in response to new international needs, and more.

ISBN: 0-87101-280-4. Item #2804. Price $26.95

(Order form on reverse side)

ORDER FORM

Title	Item #	Price	Total
__ Successful Community Leadership	2855	$25.95	_____
__ Community Building	2928	$29.95	_____
__ Organizing	1972	$32.95	_____
__ How People Get Power	2367	$20.95	_____
__ Issues in International Social Work	2804	$26.95	_____
		Subtotal	_____
	+ 10% postage and handling		_____
		Total	_____

❒ I've enclosed my check or money order for $ _____.

❒ Please charge my   ❒ NASW Visa*   ❒ Other Visa   ❒ MasterCard

_____   _____
Credit Card Number   Expiration Date

Signature _____

Use of this card generates funds in support of the social work profession.

Name_____

Address _____

City _____ State/Province _____

Country _____ Zip _____

Phone _____ E-mail _____

NASW Member # (if applicable) _____

(Please make checks payable to NASW Press. Prices are subject to change.)

NASW PRESS

P. O. Box 431
Annapolis JCT, MD 20701
USA

Credit card orders call
1-800-227-3590
(In the Metro Wash., DC, area, call 301-317-8688)
Or fax your order to 301-206-7989
Or order online at http://www.naswpress.org

Visit our Web site at http://www.naswpress.org.   SCBI98